Mary Anna
Jodi Barrows
2011

Kisses from Your Beloved

A Civil War Love Story

SAMPLER QUILT

I hope you enjoy this Civil War love story of Sadie Wilkes and Duvall Woodridge, a young couple caught up in the unrest of the Civil War. The Kisses from Your Beloved program consists of twelve 10 inch blocks and twelve love letters between our couple. This Kisses From Your Beloved sampler quilt uses two of my fabric collections, Celebrating Abe and The Pony Express. Kits may be ordered from our website, or just give us a call!

As the young lovers correspond during the years of the war, you will learn about their thoughts and feelings. I hope it expresses the entanglement of the people and the politics of the time. There are so many precursors of what brought us to the Civil War—politics, prejudices, business, the growth of a country, women's rights, rebels, and of course slavery, just to name a few. I want to present the issues as they saw them and let you come away with your own thoughts and opinions. The reasons for why and what the fighting in the Civil War was for is still a hot topic among historians today.

This story is a side bar to my family's story of the Mailly Women. For those of you reading my novels, Sadie is a cousin to Abby and Emma Wilkes. Both of these stories will come to a head at the Battle of Vicksburg during the summer of 1863. My research has been from actual Civil War letters. This is the best way to get the grass roots of how the people of the times felt about the issues. The Pearce Civil War Museum in Corsicana, Texas has a large amount of information and many letters as well. Of course, my family history passed down by the women in our family is my purest form of information as well as inspiration.

Jodi

History

The Civil War was the bloodiest war in US history. More soldiers were lost in the four year battle than all of the other wars combined. To this very day opinions vary and tempers flare over the Civil War and its causes.

The first slaves were brought to Jamestown, Virginia in 1619. Until 1806, it was legal to buy and sell slaves in the United States. Less than 5% of all slaves were brought to the states; the largest percentage went to Brazil, Spanish Empire, British West Indies and the French West Indies with the US coming in 5th.

Slavery in the North died out because of cheap immigrant labor, while it continued to grow in the South and became a way of life in the plantation operations.

In 1820 Missouri became a state. This was monumental as it created an invisible line separating the United States into what we know as the Mason Dixon Line. This created an equal number of states to vote for or against slavery. Each new state brought into the Union would have the right to choose.

At this point, people on both sides became angrier and every irritation grew deeper for the next 40 years. Many renegade groups such as the one organized by John Brown popped up, taking matters into their own hands. As the western territories grew and became states, battles were waged by those sympathetic to their causes. Subsequently, on January 29, 1861, when Kansas became a state it was called "Bleeding Kansas".

The country came to a boiling point with the Presidential election of 1860. Abraham Lincoln was elected with only 40% of the popular vote. Not a single southern state voted for him. His election was taken as a declaration of war to the South in December 1860. South Carolina seceded; within a few months over a dozen states had joined in the withdrawal and the Confederate States of America was created. The red, white and blue now became the blue and the gray.

In March, 1861, Lincoln vowed to protect US property and preserve the Union. And this is where the real trouble starts. At this time, Fort Sumter, South Carolina was located in enemy territory and Lincoln was forced to keep his word of preserve and protect. On April 12, Confederate forces surrounded the fort. Lincoln saw this as an act of aggression and called for 75, 000 volunteers. The lines were drawn as to what the future of the United States would be and what would be the meaning of freedom.

The South said they wanted the right to choose and were frightened that Lincoln would take that right away. They wanted the right to choose whether to own or not own slaves. Lincoln tried to come up with ideas that would settle the issues, but to no avail. One idea was for the government to buy the slaves and even ship them home. (On a side note, could this be the first bail-out idea from Congress?) Anyway, all plans or ideas were nixed and the War began at Fort Sumter in the spring of 1861. The fort could have been taken by starvation with enough time, but at 4:30 in the morning, the first shot was fired by the South from James Island. After thirty hours, the North surrendered the fort.

When President Lincoln called for the volunteers to sign up, they came eagerly. The immigrants saw a way to escape the hardships of their oppression, labor intense, and poverty life style. The Union offered a symbol of freedom and hope. Many were very prejudiced and would never have fought for the freedom of a black man. Only one out of ten had ever seen a plantation or slave. Stories are told of how Union troops marched into the south, the slaves in the fields cheering at the sign of freedom, only to be yelled at, spit upon, and ridiculed. President Abe Lincoln put the power of the pen into action in September 1862 when he issued the Emancipation Proclamation, which freed every slave of the South. It is believed that this and the battle of Antietam started the turn of events for a Northern victory.

The Emancipation Proclamation is an executive order issued by United States President Abraham Lincoln on January 1, 1863, during the American Civil War under his war powers. It proclaimed the freedom of 3.1 million of the nation's 4 million slaves, and immediately freed 50,000 of them, with the rest freed as Union armies advanced. On September 22, 1862, Lincoln announced that he would issue a formal emancipation of all slaves in any state of the Confederate States of America that did not return to Union control by January 1, 1863. None did return and the actual order, signed and issued January 1, 1863, took effect except in locations where the Union had already mostly regained control. The Proclamation made abolition a central goal of the war (in addition to reunion), angered many Northern Democrats, energized anti-slavery forces, and weakened forces in Europe that wanted to intervene to help the Confederacy. Total abolition of slavery was finalized by the Thirteenth Amendment of 1865.

(from Wikipedia, May 2011, http://en.wikipedia.org/wiki/Emancipation_Proclamation)

The Confederates won many of the battles up to the end of 1862, giving them the upper hand. Lincoln had a difficult time finding leaders that would actually fight. When Ulysses S. Grant came on board, the battles started to shift. With a chance meeting at Gettysburg on July 1, 1863 and the fall of Vicksburg in the preceding days of June, the South would never recover. President Lincoln called Vicksburg, "the key in his pocket" and so it was.

After 2,000 battles and 150 years, historians still battle over the issue of why they fought. Was it over slavery or the right for a state to choose? The chicken or the egg?

Some unusual facts that strike me were that the Union named the battles after the body of water that was closest, while the South named them after the closest city. The first real battle was called Bull Run by the North and Manassas by the South. Also, most of the battles were in the south, so most soldiers were buried in the south. All government ordained Civil War cemeteries are full of Union dead—no Confederate soldiers are buried there. They were considered the enemy, so none of their dead could be buried in a civil war cemetery.

The End of an Era

Sherman was one of the few who predicted the long lasting war and what it would cost the nation. After 4 years of fighting, 81 billion dollars and almost 700,000 dead in 10,000 battles and skirmishes, the war fought with untrained volunteers and enthusiasm came to a close. 1 in 5 of those soldiers would never go home again. Those who survived did so by their belief and determination.

By the winter of 1863, Lincoln had everything leaning in his direction. Officers were actually getting along and were not afraid to go into battle. Supplies, industry and manpower were readily available to him. In reality, it should not have taken another two years to put the nail in the coffin.

The Confederate Army was in tatters by the end of 1863. They were out of everything but the worst was spirit, as their heart had been broken during the past summer at Vicksburg and Gettysburg. This was the beginning of the end for the South.

The beautiful countryside of the South was stripped down, burned up and bled upon. The actions of 3 million fighting over a 4 year time period had taken its toll. Disease and devastation was everywhere. Nothing could be produced, planted, bartered, shipped in or shipped out. The entire economy had to be rebuilt.

Hopelessness and hardship led to hundreds of Confederates deserting every day during the last two years of the war. When they returned home, they literally had to pick up the pieces of devastation, poverty and the evacuation of a society. Confederate money was worthless and not accepted as legal tender. Taxes and loans were due after four years of exemption during the war and anything of value was given in the war effort. Church bells were melted into cannons and common household metals were turned into bullets.

By the end of the war, 66 percent of the Southern wealth was lost and over 500,000 farms, plantations and businesses were insolvent. Also, there were close to 4 million slaves out of work, out of food, homeless and mostly uneducated.

While politicians in Washington D.C. were busy passing reconstruction laws after the war, the South remained in upheaval as the ruined economy tried to accommodate the ensured troubles. Congress wanted to know what would become of the rebel states and the citizenship of the men who supported them. Lincoln started as early as 1863 with the reconstruction laws, but skeptics of southern intentions demanded more. Secession had destroyed statehood rights and the Confederate states would have to become colonies again, earning their rights back as states. The right of a state to simply restore its previous established powers was to reward treason and thus considered unacceptable. Confederate President Jefferson Davis was imprisoned for two years, then released after northern sympathizers paid a healthy fee for his freedom. Only one confederate, Henry Wirz, Commander of the Andersonville Prison camp was held on treason and executed for war crimes.

The horrific Civil War had the opportunity to crumble a young nation but instead allowed it to mold and shape into the nation we know today.

February 1861

Letter One

My Dearest Duvall,

I have been so sad since you left to fight the Yankees. I haven't been able to concentrate on anything. My books lay unopened and my sewing is untouched. When I close my eyes, I feel the warmth of your hand at my waist. My hand brushed your hair from your sweet brown eyes and you kissed me, unashamed for anyone to see.

We stood at the garden gate, on the cobble stone path, as we stated our love for each other. Oh, my sweet Duvall, I am worried you will forget me.

You looked so smart as you walked away. I waited at the gate until you had completely vanished from view. My heart throbbed when you turned back to see me once more.

I know they say that this war will only last a few weeks, but it will surely be the worst days of my life. I will wait at the gate for your letter to come and I will be on the cobblestone waiting for your return.

Kisses from your beloved,

Sadie

Spring 1861

Letter Two

My Sweetest Sadie,

I met up with a group of young men just like me. I never in my life experienced such noisy enthusiasm and optimism. Each soldier was frantic with delight and it was contagious.

Pres. Jeff Davis has called for 100,000 volunteers to form a Southern resistance. We answer this call for a variety of reasons. Some come for adventure, honor or duty. But I see it as the holy cause of Southern freedom. I fight for our state's rights of sovereignty; I fight for our way of life.

Our hopes are the highest that we will skunk those blue bellied Yankees in the shortest of time. Lincoln has no skills in military action or organization. The Union knows not what they fight for. Most Northern soldiers have never laid eyes upon a Negro slave and harbor their own prejudices against these black people while they fight to end their slavery. This certainly is a prickly pear.

I see not the difference in the Southern slave and the European immigrants enslaved in the work house and factory of the North. Their conditions are certainly less desirable. As they care not for the immigrant life, as they have no investment in them and can replace them instantaneously.

Our brigadier has received word that we will soon see our first action as Lincoln has sent Union forces to Charleston. South Carolina to be the first to succeed has caused a commotion in the fact that Union forces are holed up in Fort Sumter. Good ole Jeff Davis is looking for a surrender by starving them out.

Sadie, I don't know when my letter will reach you or your letters to me, but please know that you are the first thought as I wake each morn and when I rest my head each night. Look up to the moon and know that I am looking up to you t[o]o. My greatest love is all yours. Be safe and strong. I will return soon.

Kisses from your beloved,

Duvall

Summer 1861

Letter Three

My Sweetest Sadie,

I am now in my Confederate camp at Coon Ridge. We have been outfitted with right smart uniforms, weapons and ammunition. Our battle flag is complete—it was stitched by a local patriotic women's group. I thought of you and what a fine job you and your friends would have done on our flag.

It's not too exciting in our camp. Our duties range from daily drills to standing guard. Some fellows don't take the guard duty serious when the Yankees are so many miles away. We have daily living chores such as chopping wood, hauling water, cleaning clothes and the likes. Some babble about it like it is woman's work. At least it is something to do as we look for ways to pass the time. We do share books, play cards, write letters and some fight. The boredom is handled in different ways.

Our ideas about fighting may soon be forgotten when we see the eyes of the Yankees. These fellows are so young they know not what we face in the days ahead. Rumor has it that we shall soon see. Our battalion is expecting orders to proceed on.

I had to hurry and put my things away as we were called to hurry and pack camp. So now I'm finishing my letter to you with more news and our first southern victory!

We saw our first battle at a stream in Virginia called Bull Run, close to Manassas. The Yanks thought they would be the victor and an audience gathered on the hillside to watch with much ado. The Yankees were aggressive and steam-rolled us with fierce fighting by late afternoon. Then, our General Stonewall Jackson said, "yell like the devil, boys" and we pushed them back with our own heated advancement.

The strangest of events happened then. As the Yankees started to retreat, they found themselves all tangled up with the spectators and their carriages on the hill. Those yellow bellied Yankees left all their belongings, turned tail and ran away. Then, the civilian spectators with panicked looking faces turned tail and ran, too!

Oh, Sadie, with successes like this I will be back home with you before you know it. I received your letter and it saddens my heart to hear of your low disposition. Please pick up your spirit. I want you to enjoy your days with your sewing and your books. Do not be sad because of me. Your love is secure in my heart. I too wait for the day when we will be merry again.

Are you looking at the moon and thinking of me looking too?

Kisses from your beloved,

Duvall

Fall 1861

Letter Four

My Dearest Duvall,

I have received both of your letters with great excitement. I jumped with joy as I held them in my hand. My fingers trembled as I hastily opened each one. I calmed myself as to not rip the pages, as I knew that I would want to read them over and over again. At first I read so quickly the words leaping from their page. Each day I wondered what your existence was and how you were fairing. I so worried over your plight.

We too have heard of the Southern victories and the reports of the battle of Manasses. The Union called it the battle of Bull Run and Lincoln's boys are all roused up and humiliated over the defeat. He has called for fifty thousand more volunteers. Although our brave fighting boys continue to win at Wilson's Creek and Leesburg.

The papers are reporting on the yell that you spoke about. They are calling it the rebel yell and describing it as a banshee squall as they charge into battle, scaring the wits out of the blue bellied Northerners before a shot is fired. My spirit swelled with pride as I read on and my backbone quivered as I thought of its terrifying consequence.

I must confess that I cried as my fingers caressed your handwriting. I am doing well but I miss you so. I promise to keep my disposition so you can remain proud of me. I have lifted my spirit and am back to my sewing. I am working on a quilt block in honor of the rebel yell, calling it Devil's Gate.

I am using a very pretty black piece with another black shading on top of it. Although it is morbid as my friend Mary Gail gave me the scraps from a morning gown she has completed. Her Papa was mortally wounded at the battle of Leesburg. She weeps each day and has certainly brought the finality of this wicked war to our doorstep.

Stay well and yes I am watching for the moon too.

Kisses from your beloved,

Sadie

Winter 1861

Letter Five

My Dearest Durall,

You wouldn't believe the chain of events that I heard with my own ears! I hurried upstairs to write it all down, fearful I would forget.

You remember my Uncle John, father's only brother? His daughters are my cousins Abby and Emma? They went to Louisiana to be with their Mailly cousins on their mother's side a few years ago and then took a wagon train west. It was quite a scandal as Father says. They wanted me to go, but Father put his foot down good! He said no un-chaperoned group of women had business doing what they did. Uncle John seemed happy to rid himself of his daughters.

It was adventurous but quite frankly I was frightened with their plan. I do hear from them on occasion and all is well. They still ask me to come. They say I should get away from Father's rule, but he isn't as tyrannical as their Papa. After all, I wouldn't have met you if I had gone.

Anyway back to what I'm writing about. Uncle John, along with some other Southern gentleman had gathered for dinner at our house. Father wanted to show me off, so I helped with after dinner brandy and overheard all of this.

Uncle John said that one out of eight men are black, but in the south they out-number the whites. They all started talking at once about the slaves rebelling and killing us all! This rumor as well as others has shaken me to the core of my being. I can't imagine this happening.

We had gone into Vicksburg just the day before and what I saw still lingers in my mind. Some runaway slaves had been captured and were literally drug through the streets as a warning to others. I turned away from their bruised and bloodied faces. People continued to yell and throw rocks. I wondered who the rocks were meant for—the captives or their keepers. I have heard of this abuse but have never witnessed it. Mankind has got to be the cruelest animal of all.

But, Duvall, how can the South survive without the slave labor? If they are freed can we ever live in harmony? Where will four million freed slaves go to live and work? Abe Lincoln said the government would pay to free them, even send them back to their homes. There seems to be no answers and plans are going nowhere.

Uncle John and the men talked about how the world is out of control with all sorts of social changes, massive immigrants, gold fever, women's rights (which I haven't even written about), and that new telegraph which accelerates our daily life. They ended the evening saying that the two party system is as dead as Andrew Jackson. Lincoln's new Republican nation supports progress and fights against slavery, although he doesn't demonize the South. He firmly opposes the radical abolitionists and their terrorist activities.

While listening intently with my ear pressed to the crack in the door, I almost got my hair caught. I had to hurry back to my quilting, lest I get discovered eaves dropping. I am working on the quilt I call Sadie's Star. I can't wait to show it to you.

I won't allow myself to be frightened by the unrest surrounding us. Please, my love, come home safe. I need you!

Kisses from your beloved,

Sadie

Spring 1862

Letter Six

My Sweetest Sadie,

I woke this morning to the bugler sounding out his daily call. I slept so soundly after marching two days through the most splendid countryside with rich valleys of magnificent trees and beautiful, groomed plantations. My heart sang with joy at what I saw. I have such sweet memories of our beautiful Mississippi, of home, and of my sweetheart waiting for me on her white front porch. When I closed my eyes for a moment, I saw you standing there.

The sounds of the slaves working in the field jolted me back to the present. It hit me right then and there and washed over me like a wave. We fight for our freedom, the freedom to take away the freedom of another. As we were commanded to march again, my eyes stayed on the workers in the field and I realized that there would be no solution to this war, no agreement. The South will fight to its bloody death as the North and the South will not give in or give up on this thing called Slavery.

Sadie, I do not see me coming home soon or possibly at all. There is no end to man's plight. I cannot quit or give in or run away. My honor, even if in disagreement will not allow. I am a dead man on either side.

We were in the battle of Shiloh, we fought against great odds, but the victory belongs to Abe and his boys.

If this is a preview it will be a dark road to victory. Grant has taken forts and progressing his way down the Mississippi into the heart of the Confederacy.

Our many complications were that we couldn't stay together. Even then we forced the Federals back. We pressed on into a hornet's nest and Johnston took a mortal wound. Their left flank collapsed and we had them on the run. Beauregard then took command and he called off our advancement with Tennessee in our sight! We were ready to follow on to our death. With an early dawn attack on us as well as exhaustion, we soon fell away.

We all worked on burying our dead as we lost close to 11,000 which was less than Grant's; one third of his 40,000 were buried.

Among our dead or missing is little Cole Strong from down the Magnolia Road, not far from my house. They said he was too young to fight and made him our flag boy when he would not return home. He poured out his life's blood for the spirit of 76 was in his heart. I could not hold back my tears and gave him a more careful burial than most received. Cole had a little basket that he would pick berries in. He gave it to me just that morning saying that he had picked extra for me. The next thing I knew he was gone.

I have tried not to write of the dead as I do not want you to have the anguish that I have seen and felt. As I look out over the field of dead to bury, I see a field of Courage.

Oh, my dear girl, what is to become of us, all of us? Try not to be fearful as we march on each day in uncertainty. Know that my love for you is stronger than ever and I long for the day of my return.

Kisses from your beloved,

Duvall

Summer 1862

Letter Seven

My Dearest Duvall,

We had a most unexpected visit. I was sitting on the porch writing letters and quilting when a whirlwind of events started to unfold.

Late in the day, a group of men on horseback came to our property. I watched them approach. They looked so smart and proud—for a moment I forgot to be frightened! Papa was quickly out of his office and on the porch. The men introduced themselves with confidence as the 8th Cavalry from Texas. I sprang to my feet, as I had heard of them. They were Terry's Texas Rangers! I had just read about them in the Vicksburg newspaper. It stated how they were the toughest and most rugged of all the mounted groups in the South!

One smartly dressed rider with a scar on his cheek, said that he hated to bother us, but that his horse was in need and could we spare something. I was so enthralled by their appearance that I don't even remember what it was he needed. Papa took the steps two at a time and led them to the barn. He also asked them to stay for the evening meal and even offered our place for them to camp at for the night.

They wanted to eat outside as it was so cool and pleasant this time of year. Papa ate with the riders and I stayed on the porch and studied their appearance and attire. I so wish I could draw what was before me. They looked as though they had been on the trail and lived as Texas plainsmen, just as the newspaper article stated. But their disposition made up for anything lacking.

They were confident men with gold chevrons on their sleeves, above the elbow and wide gold cuffs that made a point at mid-hand with two gold buttons at the bottom of the sleeve. The gold band was also at the collar and at the band of their hats. Some wore a cavalry, cowboy hat made of black felt with a shiny, five pointed star pinned on the side. Others wore a traditional stove top hat with a bill.

I heard them tell Papa that they had fought with Indians, Mexicans, and Free-stators. This was just a continuation of the battles. They carried a blue flag with the words, "Terry's Texas Rangers" at the bottom of a white circle. At the top of the flag was written "God Defend the Right".

They traveled on hope saddles and carried the minimum of gear, for speed. I saw one of their guns—a Colt .44 Dragoon. Papa said later it was a Confederate Dance Revelry and was very rare. These cavalry men didn't carry any sabers which was unusual. Terry's Texas Rangers left in the predawn hours, in the same whirlwind as they had come.

I read everything I can about this war. It makes me think that I know where you are. They call General McClellan, Little Mac and say that he is pushing towards the capital and the Mississippi. He must apply pressure to our boys in gray. But all he has done is sulk around. I'm quite proud and sure of our southern boys. Stonewall Jackson has defeated them at each turn and saved the valley for the Confederates.

Duvall, my heart grieves with the situation that you and our other boys in gray must witness on the battlefield. I am convinced that there is no peace for us in the Union and this is the only thing for us to do. I constantly wish to have you with me as it is so hard to be separated for such a long time. Be strong of heart and know that I am praying for your swift and safe return.

All my love and Kisses from your beloved,

Sadie

Winter 1862-63

Letter Eight

My Sweetest Sadie,

I cannot write a love letter today as broken hearted widows, mothers and orphans overpower my thoughts. I hear the moans of our boys continuously. The sight of the dead and dying flood my soul with grief. Today your soldier would rather be dead. I have not written for I had no other thoughts than this.

We were all cheering as they gave the call to attack. The rebel yell never sounded better. The Yankees got a good thrashing last August at Cedar Mountain by Stonewall Jackson and in Fredericksburg this December. Our resistance continued and delivered hearty blows. With Lincoln's men, Pope and McClellan, fighting among themselves, he was definitely looking for a victory and that's when we got in the bulls eye.

We were at Antietam Creek by Sharpsburg. Along those banks we had the bloodiest days of the war thus far. The battle raged for hours. I saw things I could never put on paper. Lee and McClellan pushed their troops unendingly at each other. With nightfall and exhaustion we were unable to continue the slaughter. We suffered great losses—10,000 dead from our 50,000 and for McClellan, 12,000 of his 85,000 dead. The water in the creek ran red. It was left as a grave yard of brave fighting boys from both sides of the war.

We have survived almost two years of assaults from the Union and have had many victories, too. We planned rolling attacks in Murfreesboro; the entire right flank gave way, clear to Nashville pike almost 2 miles. Some of our rebel brigades got chewed up at the Round River and Stone River. Both sides took a good beating that first day. The next two days we fought in bone chilling rain. Again we lost 10,000 of our 50,000 and they lost 13,000 of their 60,000. We will spend the winter licking our wounds.

My sweet girl, I'm so sorry to pour out my burdens on you. But I do feel slightly relieved at doing so. Do pray for me and the other boys in gray. If our bodies survive, I'm not sure our minds will also. I long for the days of our youth, now so long forgotten.

Kisses from your beloved,

Duvall

Spring 1863

Letter Nine

My Dearest Duvall,

It seems so long ago that President Jeff Davis called for the 100,000 volunteers. When merchants dropped their ledgers and colleges suspended classes. Oh, to only have those worries upon us. No crops are in the fields. We have no hands to attend them if there were. My hostilities deepen toward the scum of the North.

We must have faith in the justices of our cause—to defend our homes, property and independence. We must fight, for we see no difference. If we should suffer ourselves by the Yankees of the North, our property would be confiscated by a tyrannical government and our people reduced to the most objected bondage.

These days I do not sew or read to pass the time, as trouble abounds and thorns are innumerable. It is a daily existence of chores and survival. Our faith and trust must not waver. Gone are the carefree days of our youth.

Our population is small with no manufacturing. We are short of manpower and military supply. Our crops are gone as well as our railroad. But we still have fight left in us till the bitter end.

All of Papa's slaves are gone except three that wanted to stay. I suspect they are as frightened as the rest of us. Really, I wish they would go, as we scarcely have food for ourselves. I went to the garden to see if we had missed anything or maybe by chance something was coming up on its own. I saw, by the watershed, a beautiful red star flower shining brightly on our barren land. It touched my weary hear so that I fell on my knees and cried. For several minutes my face lay my hands. I couldn't bear to pick it and bring it inside as I normal would. That simple, little flower gave me strength to know that it was living in these tough times.

Upon my exhausted soul, I write these things today. I hold tightly to your letters reading them until the pages are worn and smudged by my tears. Duvall, run away, please, run away and take me with you where the air is sweet and the land untarnished with this war!

Kisses from your beloved,

Sadie

Late Spring 1863

Letter Ten

My Dearest Duvall,

It seems senseless to write of our everyday existence when everything has changed, yet nothing is different. We wake each morning to opportunity at our fingers and hunger in our stomachs. A conscience decision must be made to enjoy each day to its fullest, no matter what is at our hand. I'm going to look at the good, not dwell on the loss.

A traveling pastor came by and we had a camp meeting on our ground. We gave him a meal and he preached on tolerance to the Union forces. He wasn't greeted with much excitement after he spoke. We had a good amount of folks who came for the preaching. Later in the day we had a rain and the heat and humidity was unyielding to human life. At least our rain buckets were full again.

Papa caught a wild boar and we had a good roast for several days and we shared it with a few others. He also had a newspaper with stories from the war, marriages and other political news. We hadn't received any written news for quite a while, as this war breathes down our neck.

We continue to sew for the Rebel boys as it is consumed immediately and very much needed. I also am doing some spelling school with some of the children, as school is no longer in session and their studies are lacking. Some see no need as the war holds their attentions. It will surely be over someday and we must not be found lacking with the abilities of our southern children.

Our prayer circle continues to roll bandages in the evenings. Where they go I know not. This group also brings news of family, friends a of course deaths. Not only had my friend Mary Gail lost her father b now her baby boy. In her grief she married an unknown soldier, home a brief time and became with child. Her new husband returned to war and left her in a fragile state. Now her sweet baby is gone too. I am not sure she will survive her grief.

Our sewing group is also collecting rags for carpet making. Every scrap of fabric is used for something. This has always been the way, but now we keep track of every thread. I must say that I had become spoiled before the war and now return to our ways of waste not want not. All arrived yesterday morning for an official quilting day. This quilt was a gift to Laura Rosenberg, she will marry her second husband very soon. He is wounded and will not go back to the battles. We do not know this man Aaron Smith, but the circle spoke well of him. She is hoping for children as she had none with her first husband. When Laura received word of his death a few weeks back she scarcely grieved and wore black a short time. Mr. Smith has known her family for a time and this war changes our habits and what is proper. Her quilt is a lovely Hunter's Star of brown and blue hues and many triangles. On this day food was brought by all and it didn't look as if food was scarce as the table was laden. Within a few minutes the quilt was stretch in the boards and the boards tied to the chair backs. We all gathered round and a blissful day was had by all. We chose not to speak of battles, death or the lack of our society, as it surely abounds just out our door. For a brief time we were in a world away from our sorrow. I hope this letter finds you safe and well and brings you to my home and heart. I wanted to write again quickly as my last was such a gloom with no glimmer of hope.

Kisses from your beloved,

Sadie

Summer 1863

Letter Eleven

My Dearest Duvall,

The war has literally arrived at our doorstep. We awake each morning to the sound of cannons. Foot soldiers were on the rocky road just west of our long plucked cotton field. I went closer to see the Yankees and to my amazement they did not look as frightening as I imagined but it didn't take long to see what was in their black hearts and lurked deep within their souls.

I was grabbed by one with dark unruly hair and then shoved to the ground by another. Just as I reached for my pearl handled revolver hidden in my apron an officer ushered the mocking boys back into place. Wickedness abounds in our once beautiful Mississippi and my resentment simmers for the blue bellies.

For weeks on end the battle of Vicksburg has raged on. After hiding what we had left of our valuables behind the barn door I forged on into the battle myself. I could no longer do nothing but shake at every cannon call. I found a safe path to move closer to the front which is all around us. The fighting continues nose to nose until the call is given to retrieve your dead and wounded. The dead cover the ground so that you could walk in any direction and not touch the ground. I have been tending our rebel boys. I am so sorry Duvall but I have seen what no lady should.

Almost every house has turned into a field hospital. I was not prepared, no lady would be, for the horror and suffering that I woul see. The air is foul of mass humans, blood and death abounds. My stomach groaned and lurched. I saw legs with no bodies and bodies with no arms. The bone saw of the doctor and screams of the men as they passed out overpowered the shelling. I wash men until the wa turns to blood and then start all over again. However, there is no time for nonsense, I have drowned my scruples and worked the best that I can. It is exhausting work and weary to my soul but I get up in the dawn and go at it again.

In the midst of this I have stumbled upon my cousin Emma Wilkes and Nellie, her black slave. Emma came home to Mississippi from Texas when she heard of our plight. I am not sure how she found Nellie or Nellie her but the three of us wash and nurse from dawn to dusk and many times all through the night.

Vicksburg is heavily fortified, the North must advance with a spade in one hand and their musket in another. The trenches they dig are miles long. If the Union can control our mighty Mississippi River they will cut the South in half denying fresh fighters and supplies. We not only battle the Yankees but disaster, hunger, disease, heat and exhaustion.

Our Rebel boys occupy points just a throw from the Union boys as cannons hurl and gunboats sputter. At some points they whiz by so fast you could catch them in your hat! We are all trapped here in Vicksburg, civilians and soldiers alike. Some are holed up in caves eating fried rat, mule meat and bread of corn and peas. This bread tastes like India rubber.

We didn't even realize that silence had finally arrived. We were so use to pushing the noise aside. Then for nearly an hour cheer after cheer went out that the battle was over. It wasn't until later that we got the news that our boys had laid down their arms and marched out in surrender. On July fourth, 1863 the siege was over. Now, only if this wicked war was finality.

The only cheerful thing I have to write is that none of the faces I wash or cover with a blanket was yours. Maybe when the gun powder settles I can find the moon again to see you looking for me too. Where are you my beloved? Is there some angel in camp caring for your wounds and asking for your name? Wherever you are I pray constantly that you are well. I know not what will become of us. Emma said we should go back to Texas with her. If I am not here helping the wounded or at what is left of my home, I will be with the Mailly women in Texas.

Kisses from your beloved,

Sadie

Fall 1863

Letter Twelve

My Sweetest Sadie,

My indications are strong that we will move on in a few days as this war continues to rage on. I feel compelled to write as this may fall under your eye when I am no more and I want you to know these things. I will not write of the battle of Gettysburg. I do not know how to live with or tell of the carnage that befell us all. For two days thousands were mowed down in open fields. For those of us that survived we wished we hadn't for now we have the memory of those who hadn't answered roll call.

My love for you is deathless, I am bound to you. I know this is true my love. Yet my perseverance to complete this existence consumes me.

The memory of our blissful moments, though brief, is with me and I am grateful to you and our God. The hope of future years, we might have to live and love overpowers me with grief.

I have heard the stories of the forty-seven day siege of Vicksburg. I am breathless over your welfare. I pray each day that you and your family are among the civilian survivors. You and I, if we are both still alive when this war is over will never be the same. With what we have lived, with our own hands and hearts, who will we be. I long to sit together on your porch swing like days of old and purge this from our souls. To be whom we will be, together.

I have banked my Confederate wage of $23.25 each month, as I have no use of it in battle or camp. I have all of my limbs still about me, but not sure if I will have half of my mind. I will have some land from my family. What I am saying, Sadie is will you be mine? Can you see fit to marry a rebel soldier like me? Will you walk to me with a beautiful bridal bouquet and pledge your love until my dying day? Sadie, will you marry me as soon as we can?

Kisses from your beloved,

Duvall

Kit Cutting Fabric List

Swatches are for representation only and may vary slightly from actual fabric.

Swatch	Fabric	Min Amt
	7051 Green Battleground	3" strip
	7053 Tan Battleground	9" strip
	7061 Red with Tan Birds on a Vine	12" strip
	7062 Tan with Blue Birds on a Vine	5" strip
	7063 Tan with Red Birds on a Vine	12" strip
	7078 Cream Gettysburg	9" strip
	7080 Mustard Gettysburg	12" strip
	7082 Green Nicknames	15" strip
	7103 Red Tone on Tone Vine	15" strip
	7104 Black Tone on Tone Vine	18" strip
	7105 Blue Tone on Tone Vine	22" strip
	7106 Brown Tone on Tone Vine	9" strip

Swatch	Fabric	Min Amt
	7107 Olive Tone on Tone Vine	3" strip
	7109 Green Tone on Tone Vine	3" strip
	7112 Red Star	6" strip cut at fold (6" x 22")
	7114 Gold Star	15" strip
	7119 Red Oath	3" strip
	7120 Green Oath	3" strip
	7123 Tan Check	9" strip
	7124 Blue Check	5" strip
	7125 Brown Check	12" strip
	7127 Red Check	5" strip
	7130 Red Scout	3" strip

These fabric amounts are for the twelve, 10 inch blocks only and does not include amounts needed for the settings or borders. Please refer to the quilt setting instructions on page 49 for more information.

How to use the 4-Patch Cross-cut Ruler

Sew two equal width strips of fabric along the length of the strips, then press open—seams out. Place the 4-Patch Ruler on your sewn strips, lining up the seam with the thick line on the middle of the ruler and clean-cut the ends.

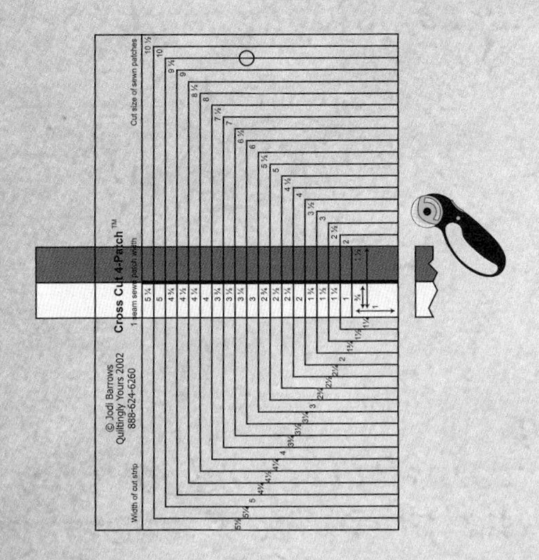

Line up your seam with the thick line on the middle of the ruler. The measurements along this line should equal half of the width of your sewn strips. Align your clean-cut edge with the desired finished size indicated by the measurements along the top or right side of the ruler and crosscut along the edge with a rotary cutter. The measurements along the bottom or left side of the ruler indicate the finished width of your section.

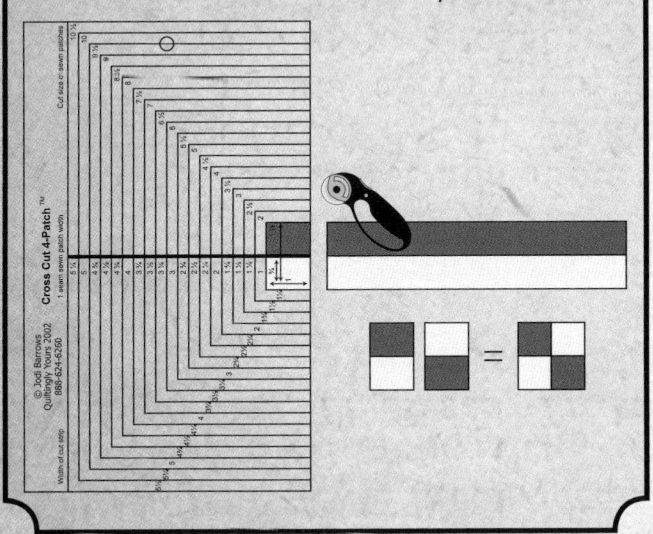

How to use the 9-Patch Cross-cut Ruler

Sew three equal width strips of fabric along the length of the strips, then press open—seams out. Place the 9-Patch Ruler on your sewn strips, lining up the top seam with the thick line on the middle of the ruler and clean-cut the ends.

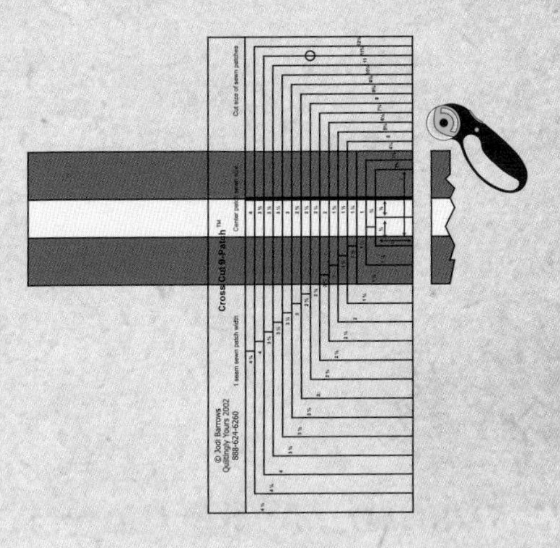

Line up the top seam with the thick line on the middle of the ruler. The measurements along the thick line should equal the width of your center strip. Align your clean-cut edge with the desired finished size indicated by the measurements along the top or right side of the ruler and crosscut along the edge of the ruler with a rotary cutter. The measurements along the farthest left side or bottom of the ruler indicate the finished width of your section. The second set of measurements on the left indicate the width of the top and bottom strips of your section.

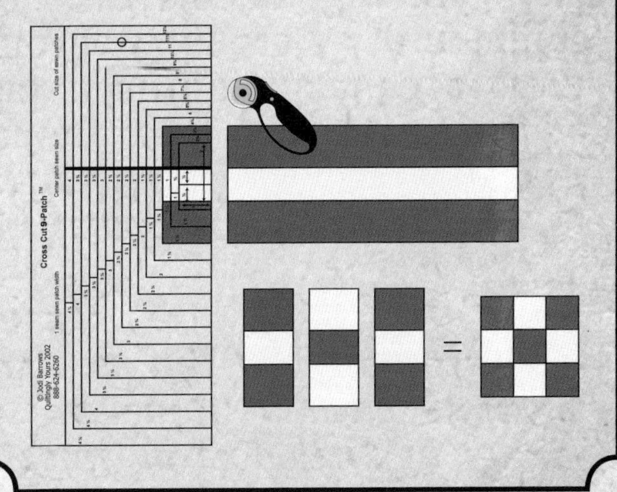

Basic Square—Option 1

The basic square will be the foundation for most of the options in the Square in a Square system.

1. Lay a surround strip face up on your sewing machine. Place the first center square face down on the strip, lining up the edges. Sew a scant ¼" along the edge of the square. Lay the next square down on the strip (only a small space between squares is needed) and continue on in a chain piecing method. Repeat for the opposite side of the square. Do not open either piece of fabric.
2. Cut the squares apart, then press open—seams out.
3. Sew short strips to the other two sides of the square and press open—seams out.
4. Cutting an Option 1 is easy using the Square in a Square® ruler. Match any corner of the center square with the corresponding angle on the ruler. Trim, leaving a ¼" seam allowance on all four sides. You may notice that the corners are sometimes blunted just a little, but this won't affect the finished square at all.
5. You now have an Option 1.

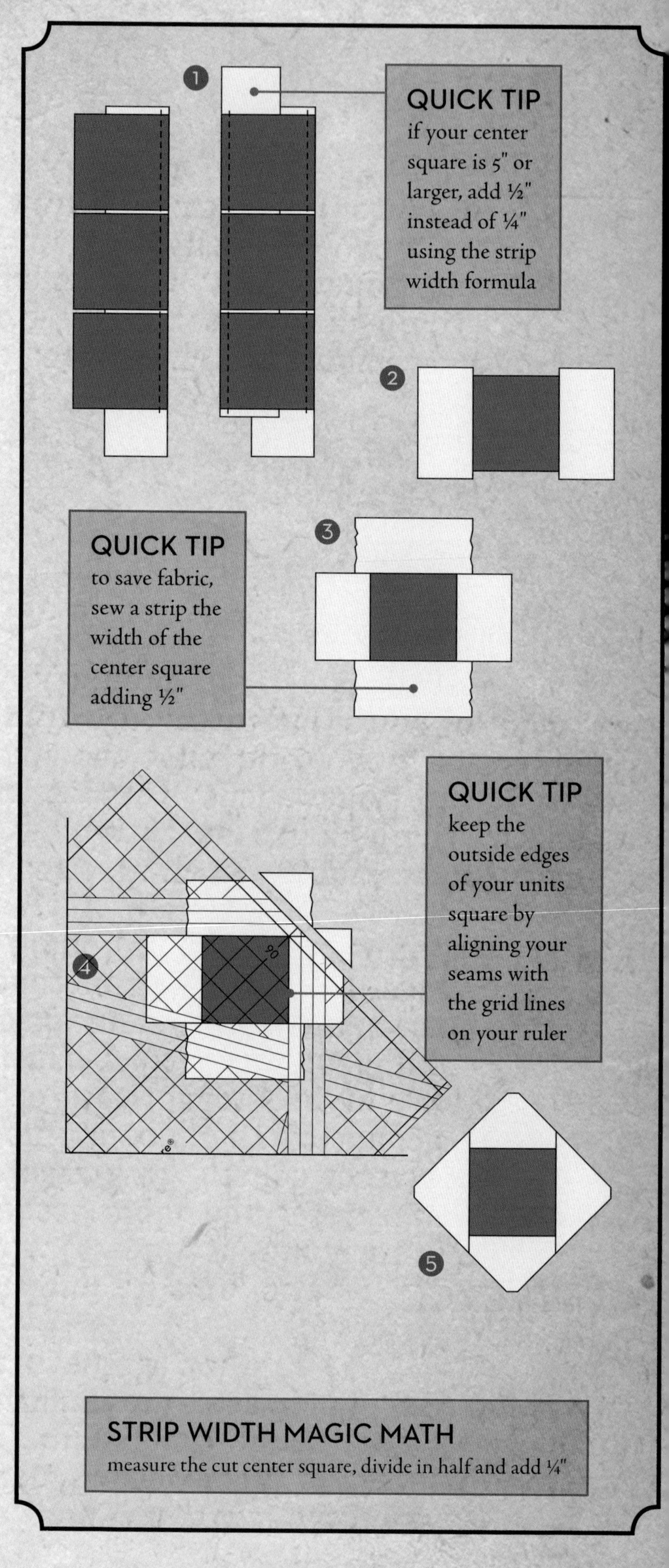

Option 3—Flying Geese

1. Sew a basic square. Trim opposing corners as you would an Option 1, leaving a ¼" seam allowance.
2. Trim the remaining corners up to the point of the center square.
3. Cut in half from tip to tip as shown.
4. You now have an Option 3—Flying Geese.

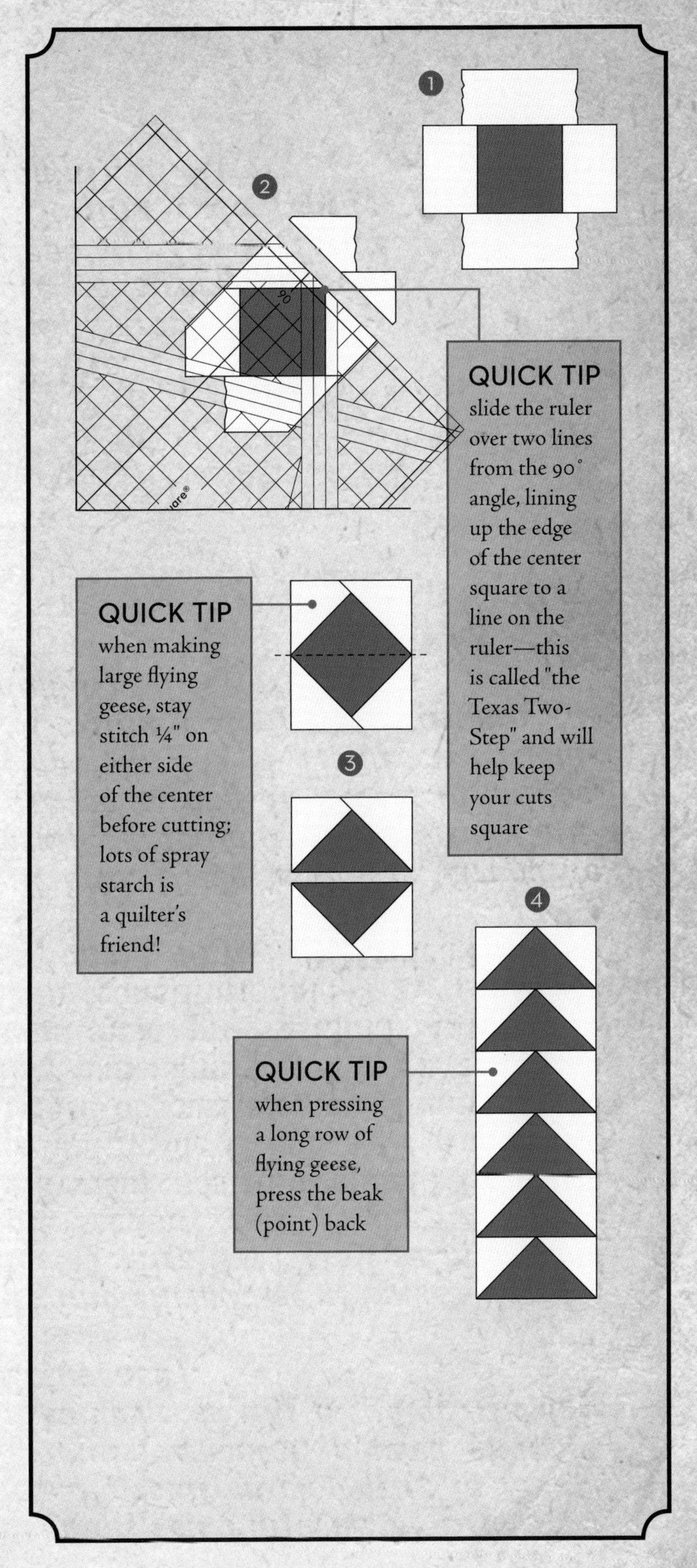

Option 4—
Half Square Triangles

You can make four half square triangle squares by cutting the option into fourths.

1. Sew a basic square using the following formula to find the size of your center square to get the desired half square triangle size: **desired half square triangle cut size × 1.414 + ½" (round up to the nearest ⅛")**. For example, if you want a 3" half square triangle (finished size 2 ½"), the formula would look like this: 3" × 1.414 + ½" = 4.742 or 4.75.
2. Trim all four corners up to the point of the center square.
3. Cut in half from tip to tip as shown to get four half square triangles.
4. You now have an Option 4—Half Square Triangles.

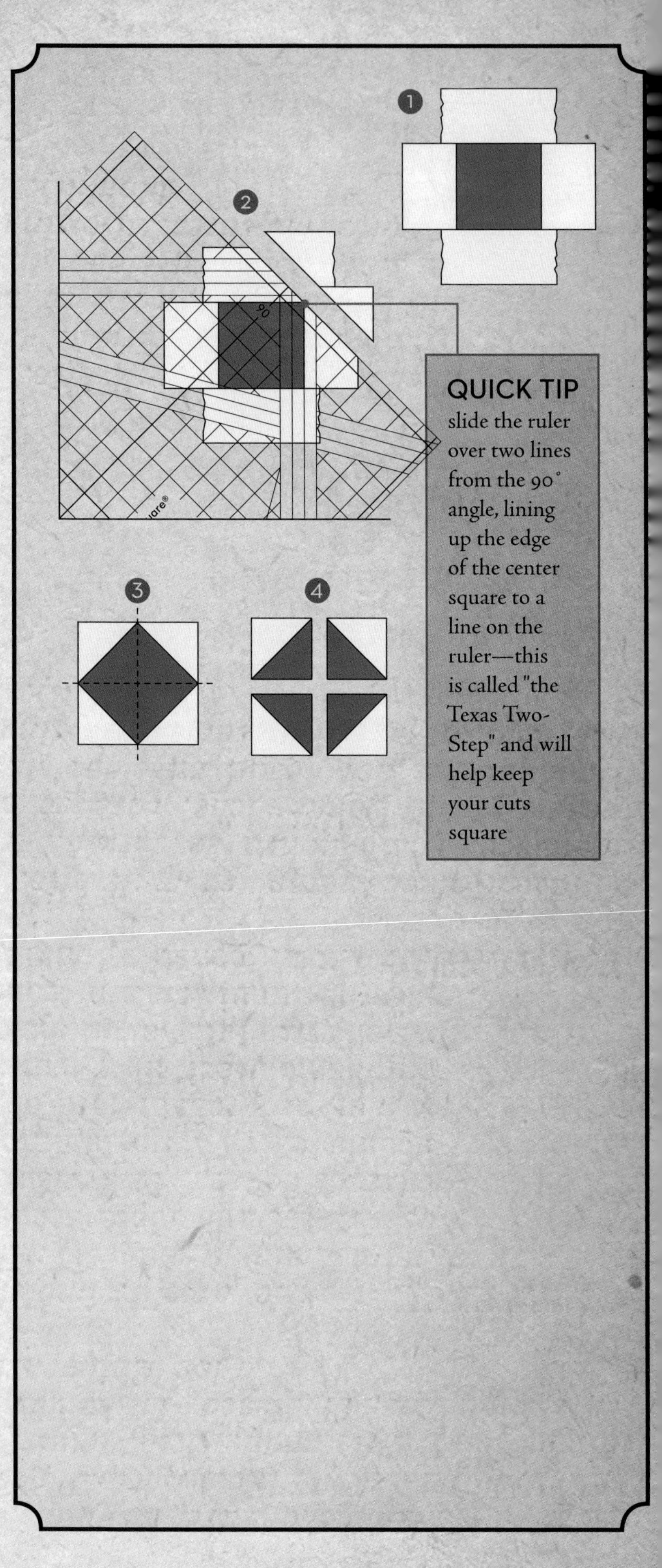

Option 11

You can make larger corner square units by combining steps from Options 1, 2 and 4.

1. Sew a basic square and trim as you would an Option 1.
2. Add a second row of surround strips like an Option 2. Trim all four corners up to the point as you would an Option 4. Be careful not to cut too much or too little. The points should be sharp.
3. Cut in half horizontally and vertically from tip to tip of the square as shown.
4. You now have an Option 11.

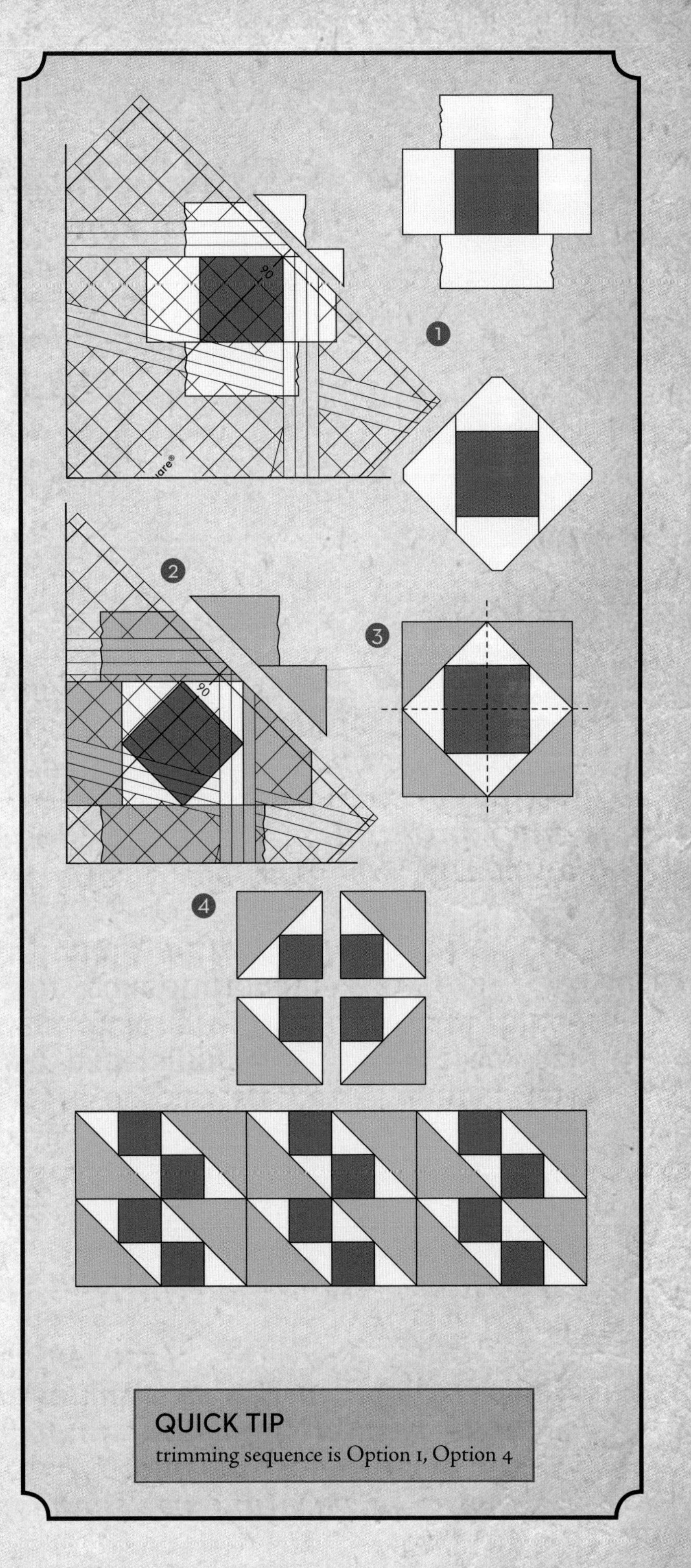

Option 14

1. Sew a basic square. Trim all four corners up to the point as you would an Option 4.
2. Add a second row of surround strips like an Option 2. Trim, leaving a ¼" seam allowance.
3. Add a third row of surround strips and trim all four corners up to the point as you would an Option 4.
4. Cut in half horizontally and vertically from tip to tip of the square as shown.
5. You now have an Option 14.

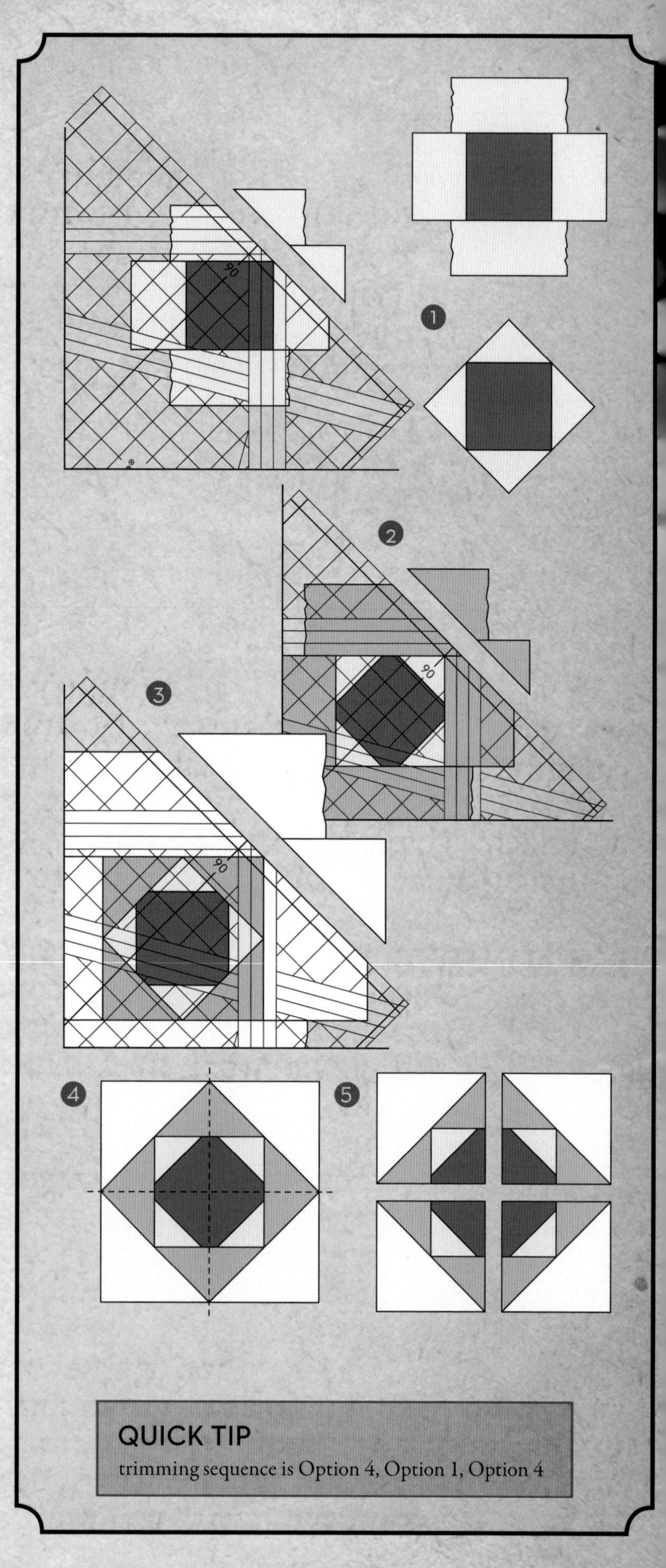

QUICK TIP

trimming sequence is Option 4, Option 1, Option 4

Option 17—Tri-Square

The tri-square is built using two equal width strips sewn together and crosscut for the center square of an Option 17.

1. Sew and cut an Option 17, using two strips as your center square. Trim all four corners up to the point.
2. Cut in half horizontally and vertically through the tips of the center square, as shown.
3. You now have an Option 17, which gives you two mirror image tri-squares and two half square triangles in different colors.

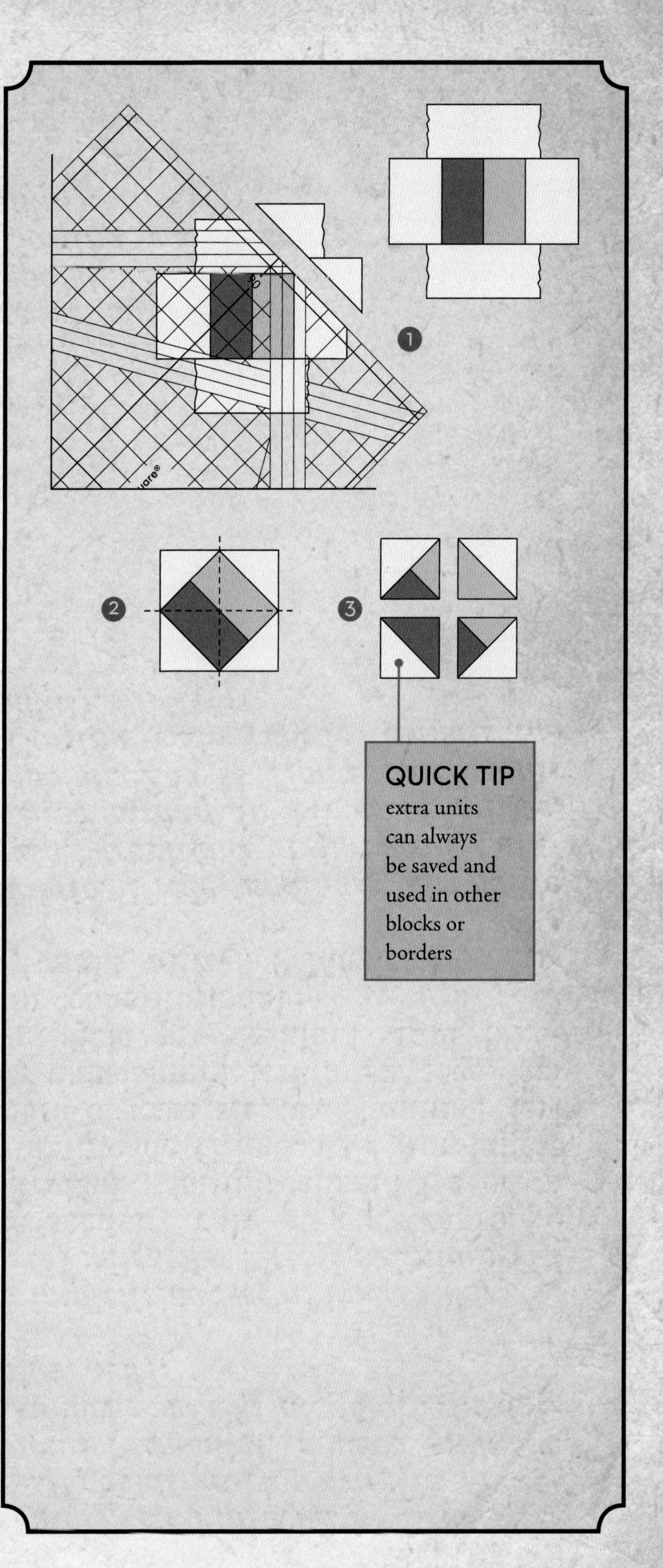

Option 39—Trumpet Square

1. Determine what size you would like your finished trumpet square to be and multiply by 2. This will give you the size of diamond you need. Sew a basic diamond.

   Place the Square in a Square® ruler on your basic diamond aligning the 120° grid line with the edge of your diamond at either 60° point. Trim up to the point of the diamond.

2. Rotate or "swing" the ruler clockwise to align the 120° line with the other edge of the same 60° point. Trim up to the point.

   Repeat for the other 60° point of the diamond.

3. Cut the unit in half horizontally from tip to tip as shown.

4. Cut several strips the same width as the surround strips used for the basic diamond. Sew the diamond halves, right sides together, along this strip or "leg", leaving a thumb space between each unit. Cut apart and press open with seams out towards the leg.

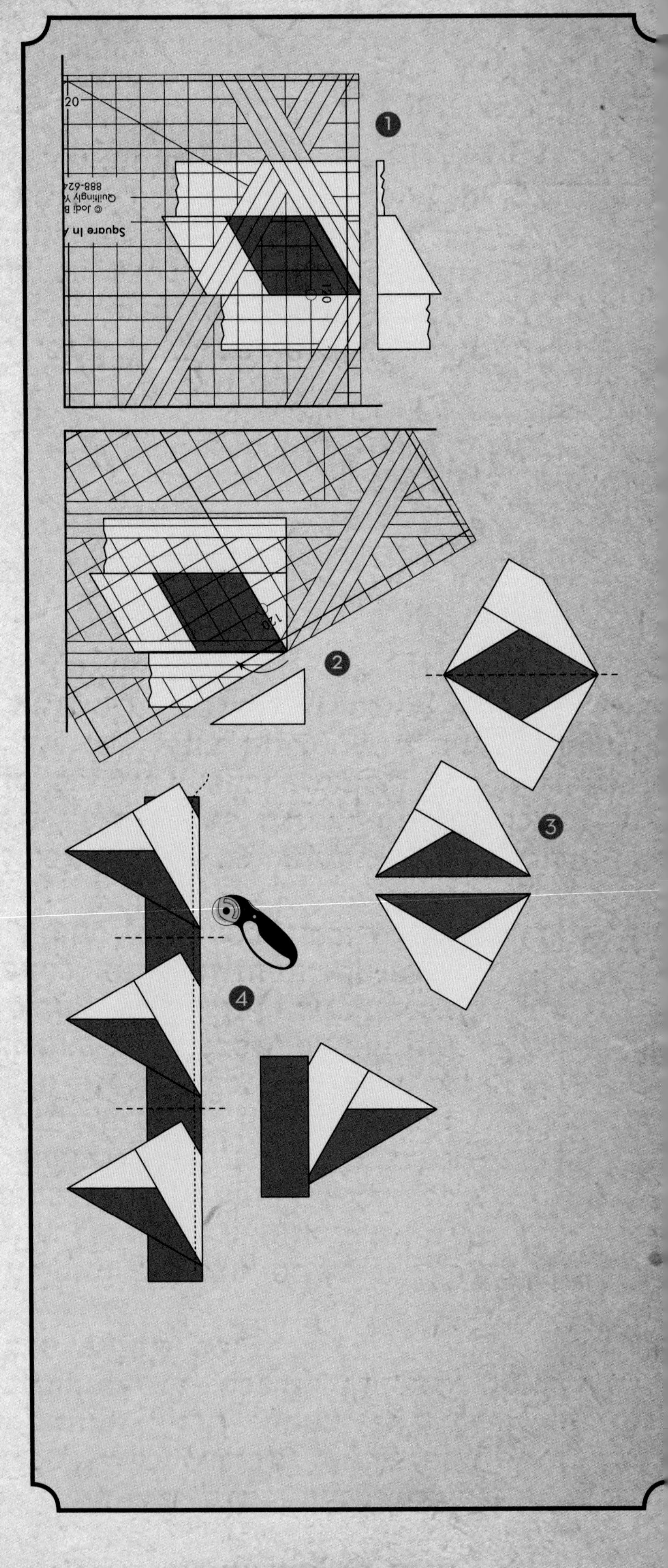

5. Repeat Step 4 with the opposite side of the unit.

6. Trim the edges of the unit, leaving a ¼" seam allowance at each point using the new square corner of the R-5 ruler.

7. Turn the piece around and lay the same square of the ruler over the fabric. The angled arrow on the square should line up with the center trumpet. The outside edges of fabric will be square and line up with the lines on the ruler on the left and bottom. The measurements on the top and right corners of the ruler should be equal over the fabric bell shape. Trim off excess fabric for a trumpet square.

   Repeat for a second trumpet square.

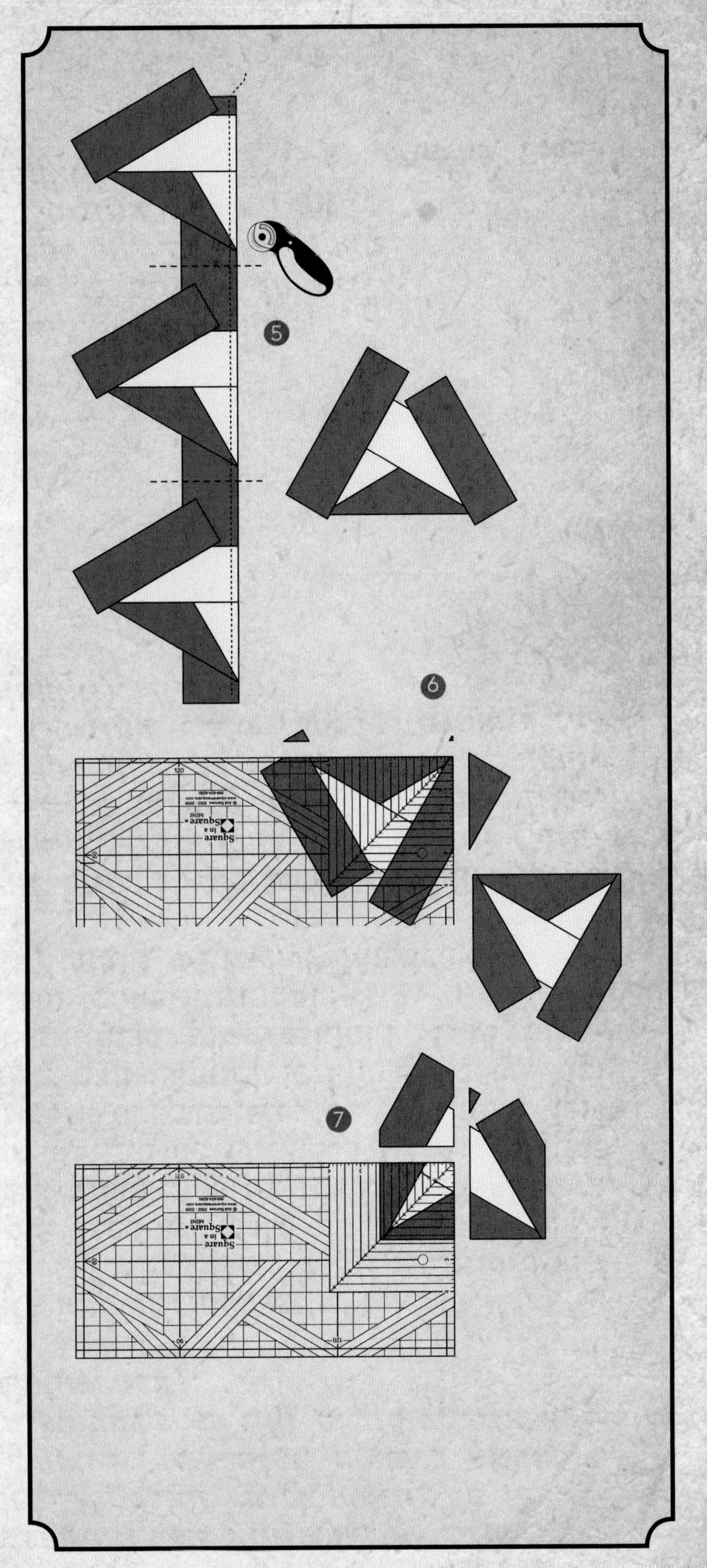

Letter One: My Cobblestone Path to You

Fabric
7105 **Blue Tone on tone Vine**
7061 **Red with Tan Birds on a Vine**
7125 **Brown Check**
7051 **Green Battleground**

Cut

Blue Vine:
(8) 2 ¼" center squares for Option 1 ❶

Red/Tan Birds:
(3) 1 ½" surround strips for Option 1 ❶

Brown Check:
(1) 1 ¾" strip for 4-Patch ❷

Green Battleground:
(1) 1 ¾" strip for 4-Patch ❷

Sew

❶ Cut and sew (8) Option 1s using a 2 ¼" center square from blue vine and 1 ½" surround strips from red/tan birds.

❷ Sew 1 ¾" strips of brown check and green together. Use the 4-Patch Ruler to crosscut the strata into 1 ¾" units. Repeat for a total of (16) units.

Sew (8) brown/green 4-Patch blocks.

❸ Sew the units from Steps 1 and 2 together in rows, alternating blocks. Repeat for a total of (4) rows.

Finished block will be (4) units across and down.

Letter Two: Prickly Pear

Fabric

7062 Tan with Blue Birds on a Vine
7103 Red Tone on tone Vine
7106 Brown Tone on tone Vine
7125 Brown Check
7127 Red Check
7082 Green Nicknames

Cut

Tan/Blue Birds:
(4) 2 ¼" center squares for Option 1 ❶
(4) 2 ⅝" center squares for Option 3 ❷❸
(4) 1 ¾" setting squares ❹
(4) 1 ¾" x 3" setting rectangles ❹

Red Vine:
(2) 1 ¾" surround strips ❶❷

Brown Vine:
(2) 1 ¾" surround strips ❶❸

Brown Check:
(2) 3" setting squares ❹

Red Check:
(2) 3" setting squares ❹

Green Nicknames:
(1) 3" setting square ❹

Sew

❶ Cut and sew (4) Option 1s using a 2 ¼" center square from tan/blue birds and 1 ¾" surround strips from red vine on adjacent sides and 1 ¾" surround strips from brown vine for the other two sides.

❷ Cut and sew (2) Option 3s using a 2 ⅝" center square from blue birds and 1 ¾" surround strips from red vine.

❸ Cut and sew (2) Option 3s using a 2 ⅝" center square from blue birds and 1 ¾" surround strips from brown vine.

❹ Sew the units from Steps 1, 2 and 3 together in rows so that you have (2) brown stars with a 3" red check center and (2) red stars with a 3" brown check center in opposite corners. Use a 3" setting square from green nicknames for the center of the block and 1 ¾" setting squares from blue birds for the four corners. Cut and use 1 ¾" x 3" setting rectangles from blue birds for the sides.

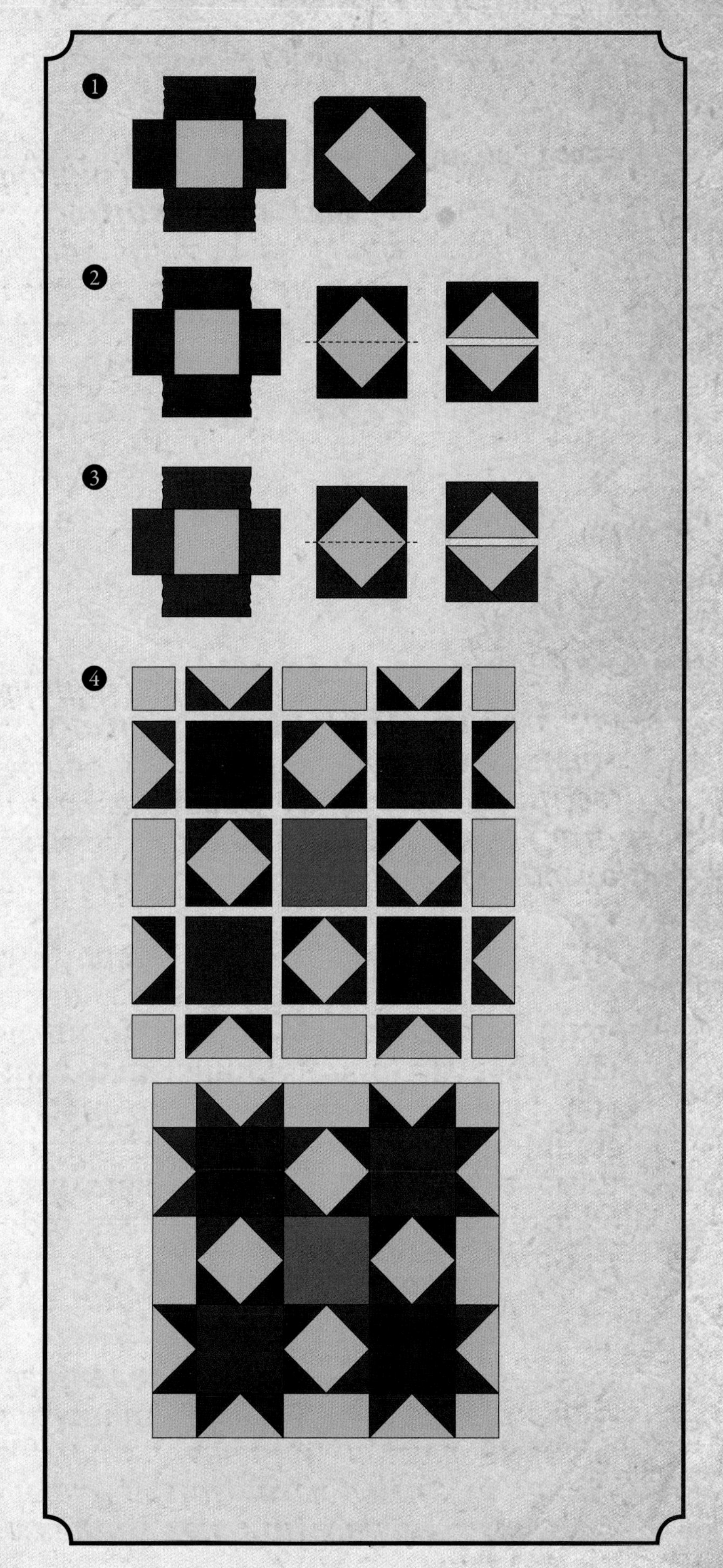

Letter Three: Coon Ridge

Fabric
7053 **Tan Battleground**
7104 **Black Tone on Tone Vine**
7080 **Mustard Gettysburg**
7082 **Green Nicknames**

Cut
Tan Battleground :
(4) 2 ¼" center squares for Option 1 ❶
(2) 4 ⅜" center squares for Option 3 ❷

Black Vine:
(1) 2 ½" surround strip for Option 3 ❷

Mustard Gettysburg:
(1) 1 ½" surround strip for Option 1 (half of length) ❶❸
(1) 1 ¾" x 18" strip for 4-Patch ❶❸

Green Nicknames:
(1) 1 ½" surround strip for Option 1 (half of length) ❶❸
(1) 1 ¾" x 18" strip for 4-Patch ❶❸

Sew

❶ Cut and sew (4) Option 1s using a 2 ¼" center square from tan battleground and 1 ½" surround strips from mustard gettysburg on opposing sides and 1 ½" surround strips from green nicknames for the other two sides.

❷ Cut and sew (2) Option 3 flying geese using a 4 ⅜" center square from tan battleground and 2 ½" surround strips from black vine.

❸ Sew 1 ¾" strips of mustard gettysburg and green nicknames together. Use the 4-Patch Ruler to crosscut the strata into 1 ¾" units. Repeat for a total of (8) units.

Sew (4) mustard/green 4-Patch blocks.

❹ Sew the units together in rows, alternating blocks.

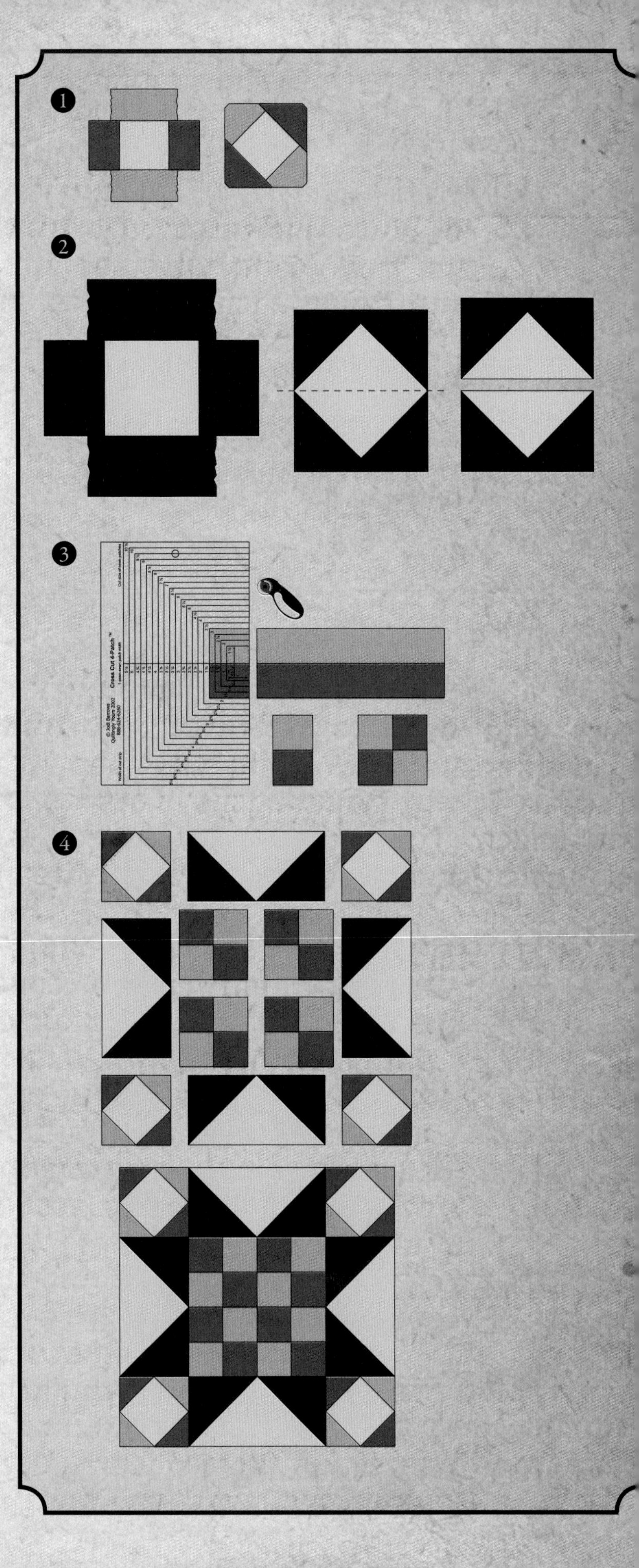

Letter Four: Devil's Gate

Fabric

7114 **Gold Star**

Various Scraps *(three 1 ½" x 3" rectangles from each of the following—7103 Red Tone on Tone Vine, 7105 Blue Tone on Tone Vine, 7109 Green Tone on Tone Vine, 7112 Red Star, 7119 Red Oath, 7120 Green Oath, 7124 Blue Check, 7127 Red Check, 7130 Red Scout—plus one from Black Vine)*

7104 **Black Tone on Tone Vine**

Cut

Gold Star:

(5) 2 ¼" center squares for Option 1 ❶
(2) 2 ⅝" center squares for Option 3 ❷
(8) 1 ¾" x 3" rectangles ❶❸

Various Scraps:

(28) 1 ½" surround strips for Options 1 and 3 ❶❷

Black Vine:

(4) 3" squares ❸
(4) 1 ¾" squares ❸

Sew

❶ Cut and sew (5) Option 1s using 2 ¼" center squares from gold star and 1 ½" surround strips from various scraps.

❷ Cut and sew (2) Option 3 flying geese using 2 ⅝" center squares from gold star and 1 ½" surround strips from various scraps.

❸ Sew block together in sections.

Letter Five: Sadie's Star

Fabric
7127 **Red Check**
7106 **Brown Tone on Tone Vine**
7063 **Tan with Red Birds on a Vine**
7103 **Red Tone on Tone Vine**

Cut
Red Check:
(1) 3 ⅜" center square for Option 1 ❶
(4) 1 ½" squares ❹

Brown Vine:
(1) 2" surround strip for Options 1 and 4 

Tan/Red Birds:
(1) 4" center square for Option 4 ❷
(2) 3 ¾" center squares for Option 3 ❸
(4) 1 ½" x 4 ½" rectangles ❹
(8) 1 ½" x 2 ½" rectangles ❹

Red Vine:
(1) 2 ¼" surround strip for Option 3 ❸

Sew

❶ Cut and sew (1) Option 1 using a 3 ⅜" center square from red check and 2" surround strips from brown vine.

❷ Cut and sew (1) Option 4 half square triangles using a 4" center square from tan/red birds and 2" surround strips from brown vine.

❸ Cut and sew (2) Option 3 flying geese using a 3 ¾" center square from tan/red birds and 2 ¼" surround strips from red vine.

❹ Sew block together in sections.

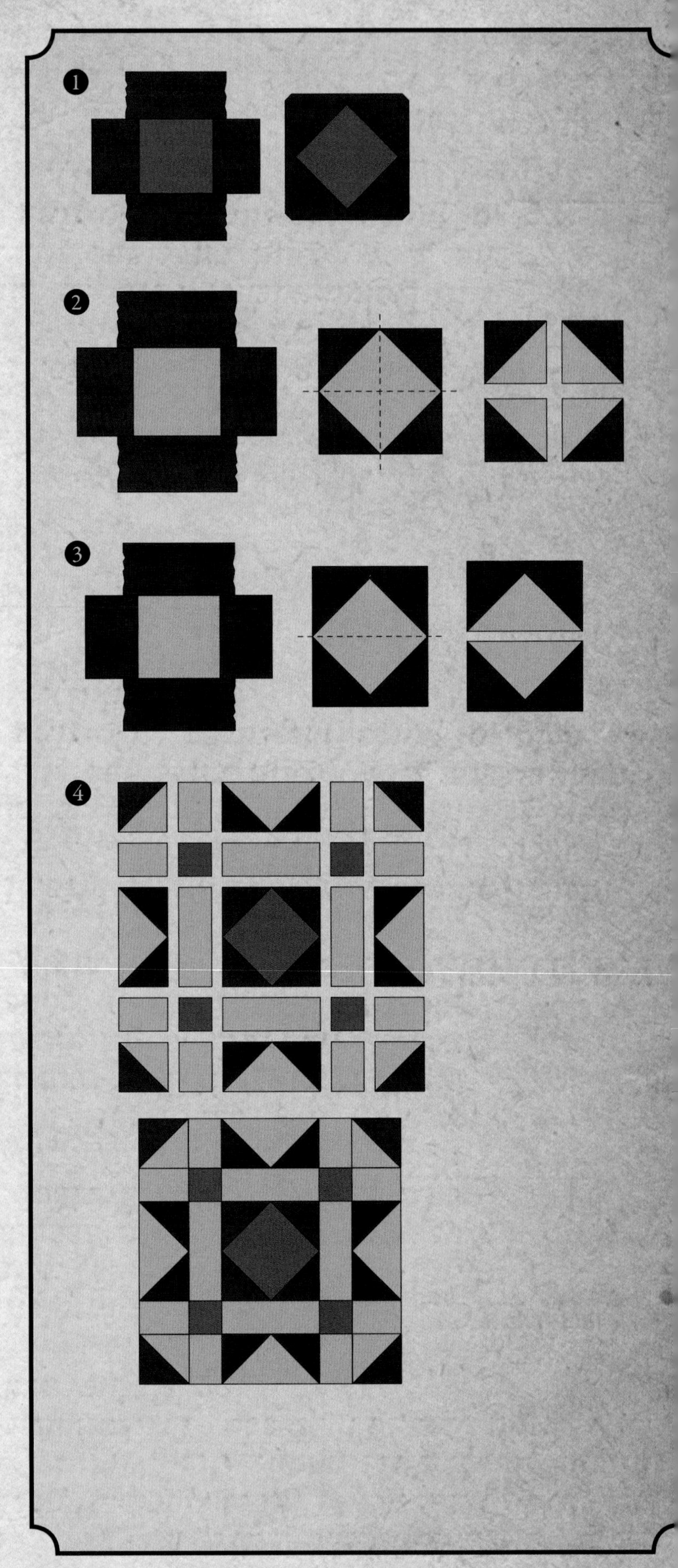

ʟetter Six: Baskets

Fabric

7114 Gold Star
7104 Black Tone on Tone Vine
7105 Blue Tone on Tone Vine
7106 Brown Tone on Tone Vine
7107 Olive Tone on Tone Vine

Cut

Gold Star:
1) 4 ¾" center square for Option 1 ❶
2) 4" center squares for Option 4 ❷
8) 2 ½" squares ❸

Black Vine:
4) 1" x 9" bias strips for basket handles ❶
1) 2 ¾" x 5" surround strips for Option 1 ❶
2) 2 ¼" x 5" surround strips for Option 4 ❷

Blue Vine:
1) 2 ¾" x 5" surround strips for Option 1 ❶
2) 2 ¼" x 5" surround strips for Option 4 ❷

Brown Vine:
1) 2 ¾" x 5" surround strips for Option 1 ❶
2) 2 ¼" x 5" surround strips for Option 4 ❷

Olive Vine:
1) 2 ¾" x 5" surround strips for Option 1 ❶
2) 2 ¼" x 5" surround strips for Option 4 ❷

Sew

❶ Cut and sew (1) Option 1 using a 4 ¾" center square from gold star and one each 2 ¾" surround strips from black vine, blue vine, brown vine and olive vine.

If you would like to add basket handles, cut 1" bias strips; then sew, trim and loop together. Tuck in as you sew the surround strips to the center square.

❷ Cut and sew (2) Option 4 half square triangles using a 4" center square from gold star and one each 2 ¼" surround strips from black vine, blue vine, brown vine and olive vine.

❸ Sew block together in sections.

Letter Seven: Whirlwind

Fabric
7103 **Red Tone on Tone Vine**
7080 **Mustard Gettysburg**
7112 **Red Star**

Cut
Red Vine:
(5) 3 ⅜" center squares for Option 4 ❶
(1) 1 ½" square ❸

Mustard Gettysburg:
(2) 2" surround strips for Option 4 ❶
(1) 3" x 30" surround strip for Option 4 ❷
(4) 1 ½" x 5" rectangles ❸

Red Star:
(1) 5 ½" center square for Option 4 ❷

Sew

❶ Cut and sew (5) Option 4 half square triangles using a 3 ⅜" center squares from red vine and 2" surround strips from mustard gettysburg.

❷ Cut and sew (1) Option 4 half square triangle using a 5 ½" center square from red star and 3" surround strips from mustard gettysburg.

❸ Sew block together in sections.

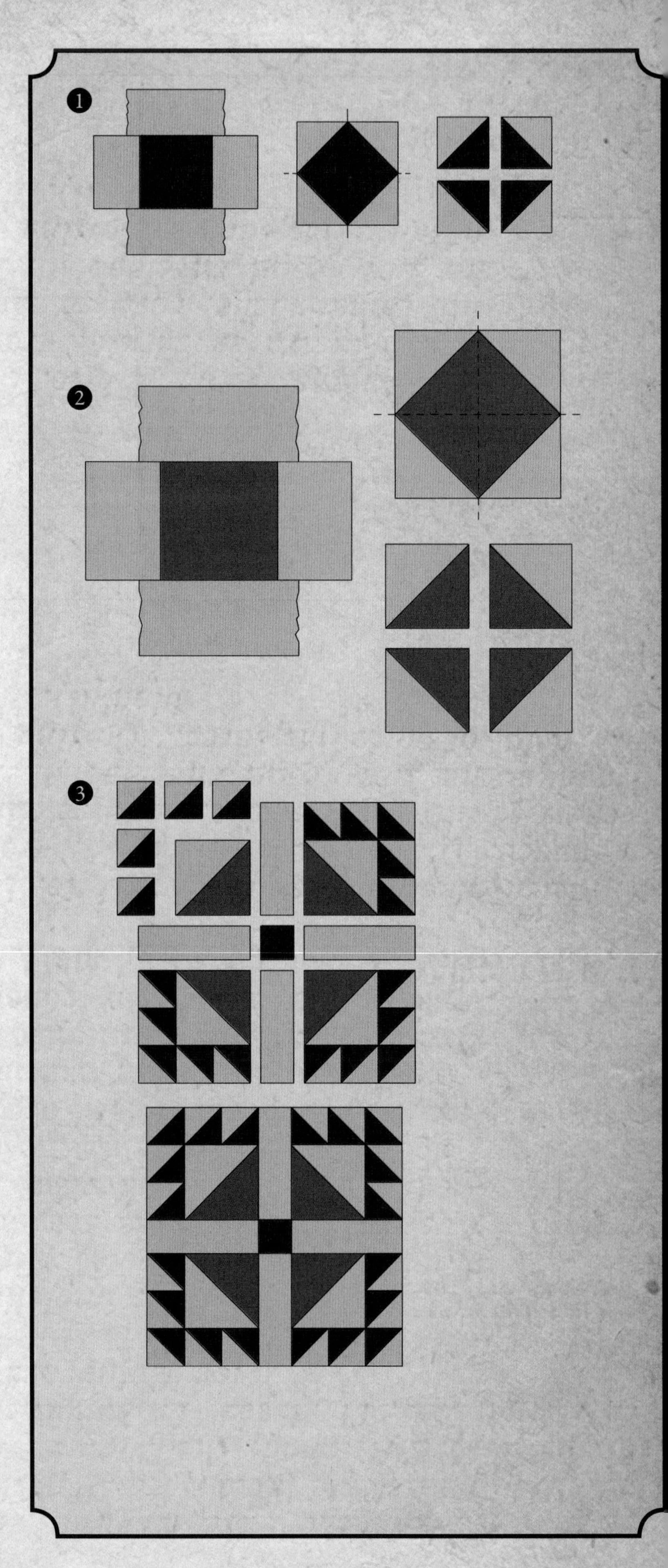

Letter Eight: Bull's Eye

Fabric
7082 Green Nicknames
7123 Tan Check
7103 Red Tone on Tone Vine
7104 Black Tone on Tone Vine

Cut
Green Nicknames:
(2) 3 ¾" center squares for Option 3 ❶
(1) 1 ½" x 10" strip for 4-Patch ❷

Tan Check:
(1) 2 ⅛" surround strips for Option 3 ❶
(1) 1 ½" x 10" strip for 4-Patch ❷
(1) 1 ½" x 12" strip for 4-Patch ❸
(1) 1 ½" x 18" strip for 4-Patch ❹
(4) 1 ½" x 4 ½" rectangles ❻
(8) 1 ½" x 2 ½" rectangles ❻

Red Vine:
(1) 1 ½" x 12" strip for 4-Patch ❸
(4) 1 ½" squares ❻

Black Vine:
(1) 1 ½" x 18" strip for 4-Patch ❹

Sew

❶ Cut and sew (2) Option 3 flying geese using 3 ¾" center squares from green nicknames and 2 ⅛" surround strips from tan check.

❷ Sew 1 ½" x 10" strips of tan check and green nicknames together. Use the 4-Patch Ruler to crosscut the strata into 1 ½" units. Repeat for a total of (2) tan/green units.

❸ Sew 1 ½" x 12" strips of tan check and red vine together. Use the 4-Patch Ruler to crosscut the strata into 1 ½" units. Repeat for a total of (6) tan/red units.

❹ Sew 1 ½" x 18" strips of tan check and black vine together. Use the 4-Patch Ruler to crosscut the strata into 1 ½" units. Repeat for a total of (8) tan/black units.

❺ Sew (2) tan/green/black 4-Patch units and (8) tan/red/black 4-Patch units

❻ Sew block together in sections.

Letter Nine: Star Flower

Fabric
7123 **Tan Check**
7103 **Red Tone on Tone Vine**
7104 **Black Tone on Tone Vine**
7082 **Green Nicknames**

Cut

Tan Check:
(4) 3" center squares for Option 3 ❶
(4) 1 ½" x 5" rectangles ❸
(4) 2" squares ❸

Red Vine:
(1) 1 ¾" x 30" surround strip for Option 3 ❶
(1) 4" center square for Option 11 ❷
(1) 1 ½" square ❸

Black Vine:
(1) 1 ¾" x 30" surround strip for Option 3 ❶
(1) 2 ¼" surround strip for Option 11, row one (half of length) ❷

Green Nicknames:
(1) 3 ¼" surround strips for Option 11, row two ❷

Sew

❶ Cut and sew (4) Option 3 flying geese using 3" center squares from tan check and 1 ¾" surround strips from red vine on adjacent sides and 1 ¾" surround strips from black vine for the other two sides. When cutting, watch color placement carefully and where you cut with the 90°. This is directional.

❷ Sew an Option 11 using a 4" center square from red vine and 2 ¼" surround strips from black vine for row one and 3 ¼" surround strips from green nicknames for row two.

❸ Sew block together in sections.

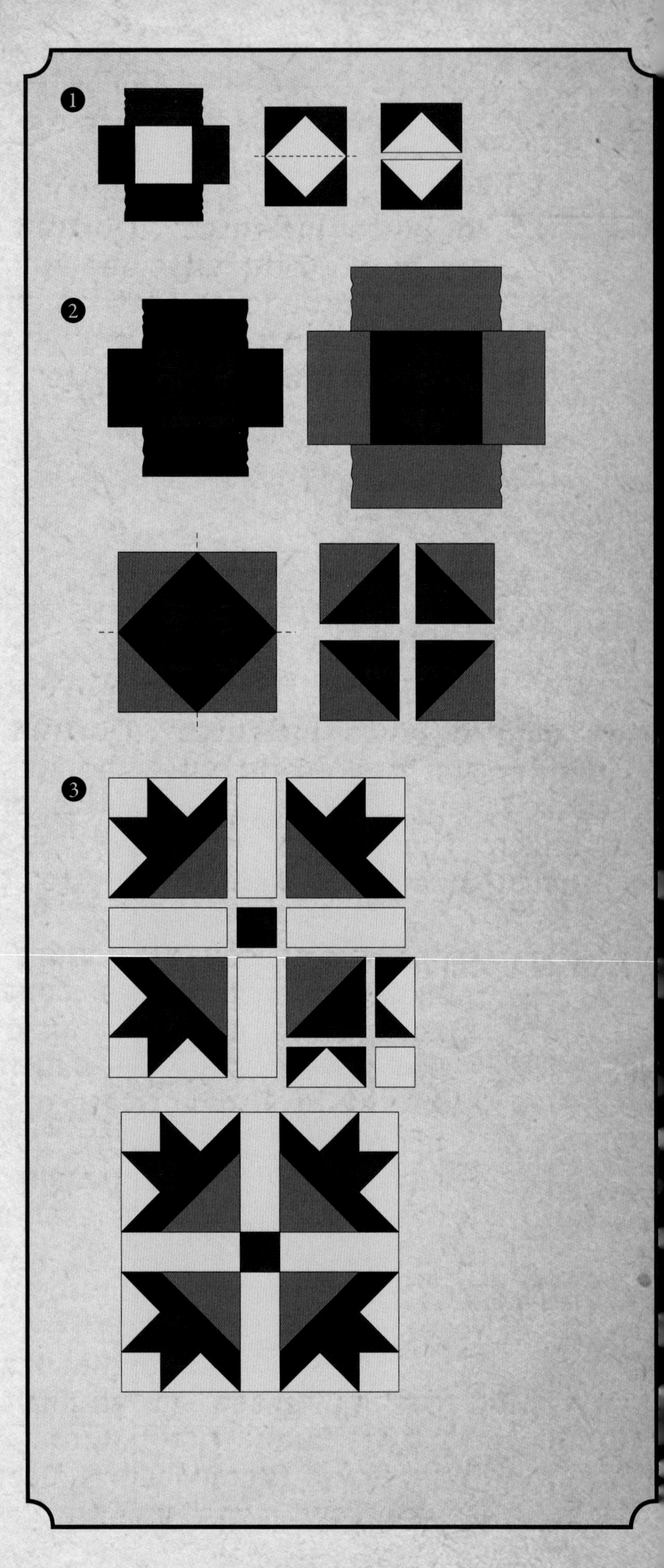

ꞁetter Ten: Hunters Star

ꞁabric

ꞁ105 Blue Tone on Tone Vine
ꞁ125 Brown Check
ꞁ078 Cream Gettysburg

ꞁut

ꞁlue Vine:
4) 3" center squares for Option 14 ❶
2) 2 ¼" surround strips for Option 14, row two ❶

ꞁrown Check:
2) 1 ¾" surround strips for Option 14, row one ❶

ꞁream Gettysburg:
2) 3" surround strips for Option 14, row three ❶

ꞁew

❶ Cut and sew (4) Option 14s using 3" center squares from blue vine and 1 ¾" surround strips from brown check for row one and 2 ¼" surround strips from blue vine for row two. Use 3" surround strips from cream gettysburg for row three.

❷ Sew block together in sections.

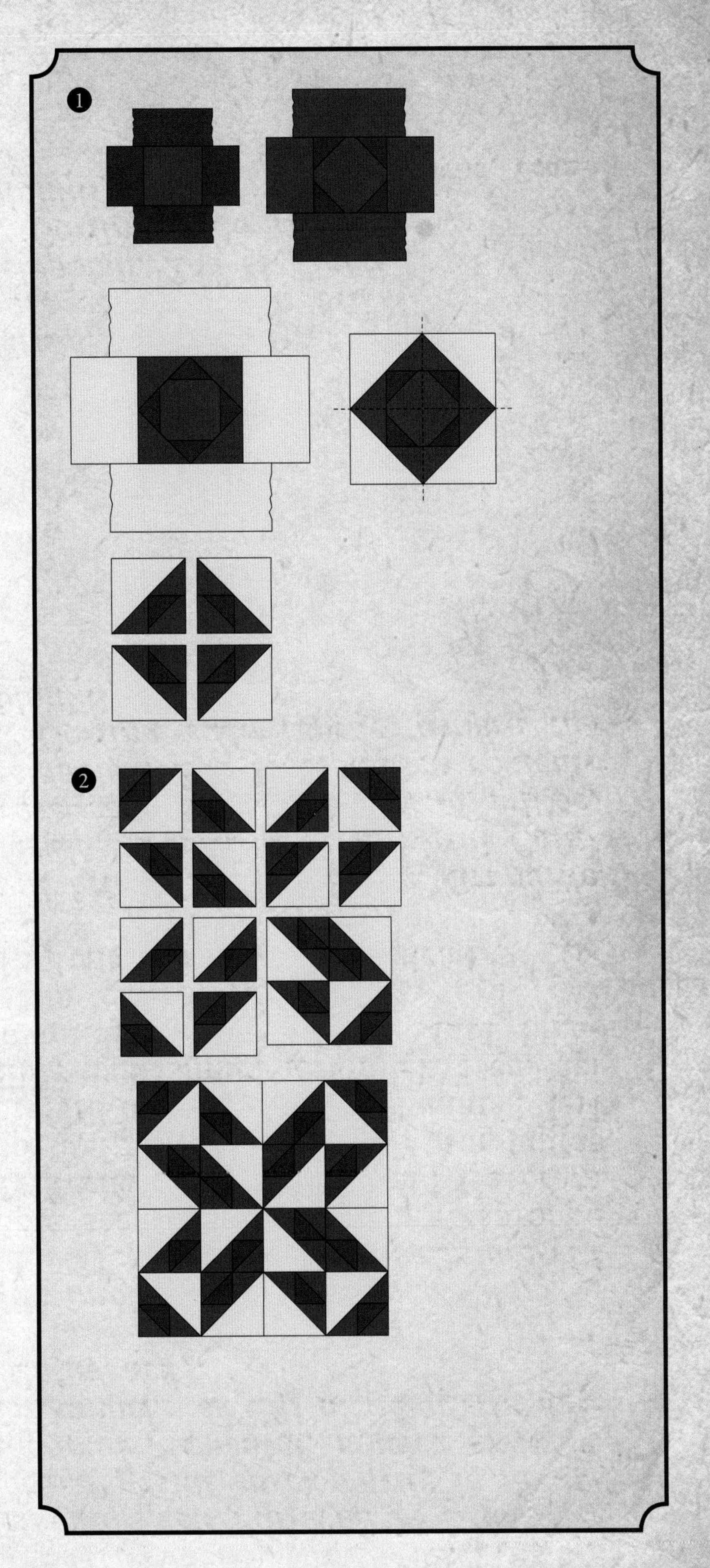

Letter Eleven: Barn Door

Fabric
7053 **Tan Battleground**
7124 **Blue Check**
7105 **Blue Tone on Tone Vine**
7061 **Red with Tan Birds on a Vine**

Cut

Tan Battleground:
(1) 2 ⅝" center square for Option 1 ❶
(1) 3" surround strip for Option 14, row two ❷
(4) 2 ¼" x 3 ½" rectangles ❸

Blue Check:
(1) 1 ¾" surround strip for Option 1 ❶

Blue Vine:
(1) 3 ⅝" center square for Option 14 ❷
(1) 3 ¾" surround strip for Option 14, row three ❷

Red/Tan Birds:
(1) 2" surround strip for Option 14, row one ❷
(4) 2 ¼" x 3 ½" rectangles ❸

Sew

❶ Cut and sew an Option 1 using a 2 ⅝" center square from tan battleground and 1 ¾" surround strips from blue check.

❷ Cut and sew an Option 14 using a 3 ⅝" center square from blue vine and 2" surround strips from red/tan birds for row one and 3" surround strips from tan battleground for row two. Use 3 ¾" surround strips from blue vine for row three.

❸ Sew block together in sections.

Letter Twelve: Bouquet

Fabric

7103 Red Tone on Tone Vine
7114 Gold Star
7109 Green Tone on Tone Vine
7105 Blue Tone on Tone Vine
7125 Brown Check
7104 Black Tone on Tone Vine

Cut

Red Vine:
(1) 2 ⅝" x 16" strip ❶
(3) 1 ¾" squares ❺

Gold Star:
(1) 2 ⅝" x 16" strip ❶
(3) 1 ¾" squares ❺
(3) 1 ¾" x 3" rectangles ❺
(1) 6 ½" center diamond for Option 39
 (you may need to cut first) ❻
(1) 3 ½" strips for leg of Option 39 ❻

Green Vine:
(4) 2 ¾" x 5" surround strips for Option 17 ❷❹

Blue Vine:
(3) 2 ¾" x 5" surround strips for Option 17 ❸

Brown Check:
(2) 2 ¾" x 5" surround strips for Option 17 ❹

Black Vine:
(1) 3 ½ " surround strip for Option 39 ❻

Sew

❶ Sew 2 ⅝" x 16" strips of red vine and gold star together. Crosscut the strata into (3) 4 ¾" units.

❷ Cut and sew an Option 17 using a 4 ¾" unit from Step 1 for the center square. Use (3) 2 ¾" x 5" rectangles from green vine and (1) 2 ¾" x 5" rectangle from a scrap piece of left over fabric for the surround strips. Watch color placement carefully.

❸ Cut and sew an Option 17 using a 4 ¾" unit from Step 1 for the center square. Use (3) 2 ¾" x 5" rectangles from blue vine and (1) 2 ¾" x 5" rectangle from a scrap piece of fabric for the surround strips. Watch color placement carefully.

❹ Cut and sew an Option 17 using a 4 ¾" unit from Step 1 for the center square. Use (2) 2 ¾" x 5" rectangles from brown check on opposing sides and (1) one each 2 ¾" x 5" rectangles from a scrap piece of fabric and green vine for the surround strips. Watch color placement carefully.

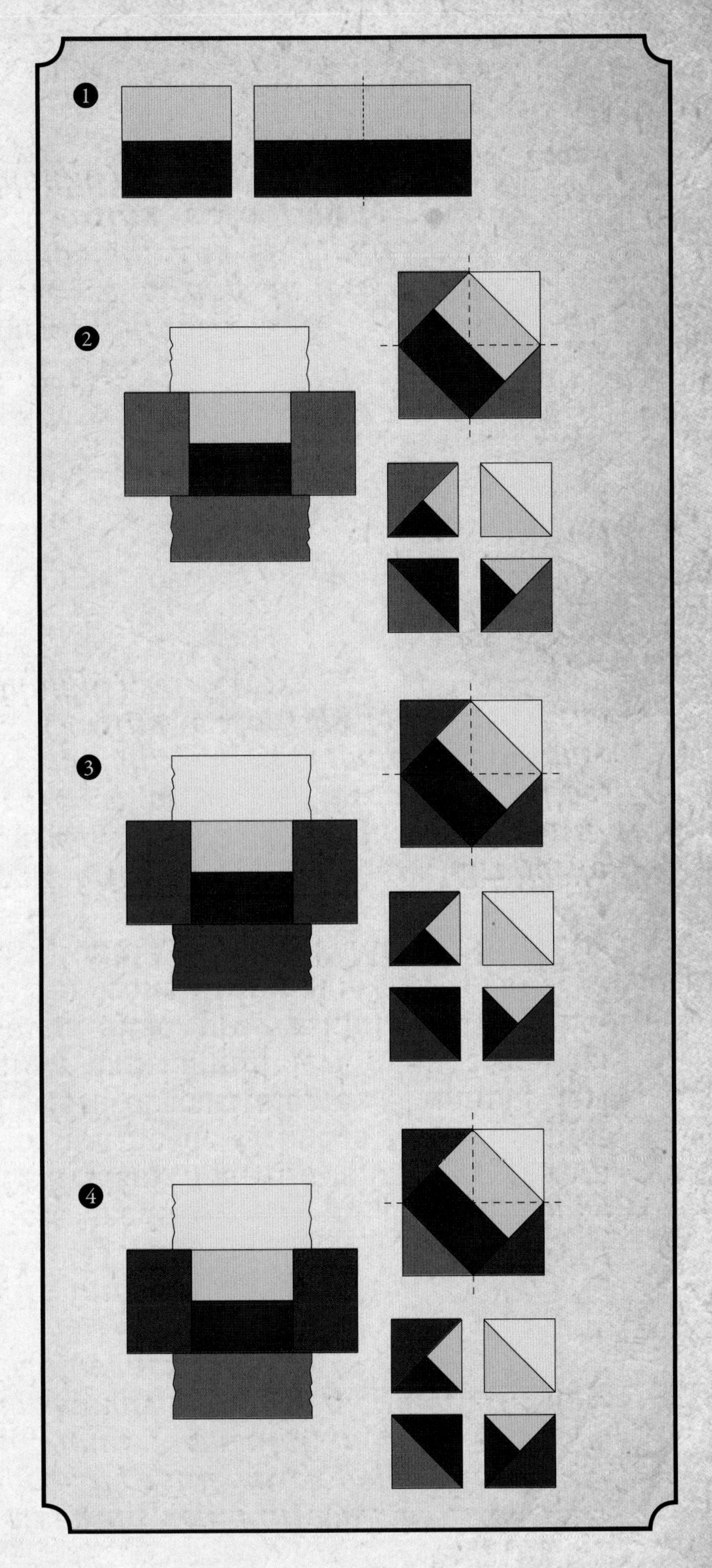

5. Sew a 1 ¾" square from red vine and a 1 ¾" square from gold star together then stitch to the long side of a 1 ¾" x 3" rectangle from gold star. Repeat for a total of (3) units.
6. Sew an Option 39 using a 6 ½" center diamond from gold star and 3 ½" surround strips from black vine. Use 3 ½" strips from gold star for the leg. Cut into a 5 ½" trumpet using the gridlines on your ruler. It is a large trumpet, but can still be completed correctly. *For additional help with the Option 39 Trumpet Square, visit squareinasquare.com for a step-by-step instructional video.*
7. Sew block together in sections.

Quilt Setting 59 x 73

Backing (4 yds), Binding (1 yd)

Fabric: Color Combo 1
7080 Mustard Gettysburg (2 yds)
7103 Red Tone on Tone Vine (2 yds)

Fabric: Color Combo 2
7078 Cream Gettysburg (2 yds)
7106 Brown Tone on Tone Vine (2 yds)

Fabric: Color Combo 3
7080 Mustard Gettysburg (2 yds)
7104 Black Tone on Tone Vine (2 yds)

Cut (from your choice of color combo)

Gettysburg:
(20) 1 ½" strips ❶❷❹
(6) 3 ½" strips for inner border ❼

Vine:
(13) 1 ½" strips ❶❷❹
(6) 3 ½" strips for inner border ❼
(6) 2 ½" strips for outer border ❼

Sew

❶ Sew a 1 ½" strip from vine to both long sides of a 1 ½" strip from gettysburg. Use the 9-Patch Ruler to crosscut the strata into 1 ½" units. Repeat as necessary for a total of (56) units.

❷ Sew a 1 ½" strip from gettysburg to both long sides of a 1 ½" strip from vine. Use the 9-Patch Ruler to crosscut the strata into 1 ½" units. Repeat as necessary for a total of (28) units.

❸ Sew a 9-Patch block together in rows using (2) units from Step 1 and (1) unit from Step 2. You should have a total of (28) vine/gettysburg blocks.

❹ Sew a 1 ½" strip from gettysburg to both long sides of a 1 ½" strip from vine. Crosscut the strata into 10 ½" units. Repeat for a total of (31) units.

❺ Sew (4) blocks from Step 3 together horizontally, alternating with (3) units from Step 4. Repeat for a total of (4) rows.

❻ Sew (4) units from Step 4 together horizontally, alternating with the completed blocks or letters from this program. Repeat for a total of (4) rows.

❼ Sew strips from Steps 5 and 6 in alternating rows.

Sew the long sides of the borders to the quilt first, then add the top and bottom. Use the remaining 9-Patch blocks from Step 3 for the four corners of both the inner borders.